A Quiet

an autobiography

Fred Gallienne

Cover Design: Vikki Gray 28 July 2019

© Fred Gallienne, 2018

First Published 2018 by the Author

ISBN 9780993515163

Printed by *Printed in Guernsey*, Vale, Guernsey, GY6 8NX

Other works by the author:

The Harassment of Mr de Bré (Guernsey-based Novel)

For my mother,

For everything she did for me.

Acknowledgements

Thank you:

....

Alfa Warring

Lisa Burton

For your support and guidance.

....

Mr Carman

The Guernsey Press

For allowing me use of your photographs.

....

Vikki Gray

For making sense of my scribblings and designing the cover.

....

An Introduction

I have been asked so many times why I hadn't written about the Occupation. I heard it said that it was about time another book be written by a Guernsey-born person who survived the Occupation on the Island and can give accurate descriptions of what it was like for a young person then.

This is that book.

Not only does it describe my time on the Island during the Occupation but also my childhood in Guernsey before the war and the years in the growing industry that followed later on – a subject I am asked about nearly as often.

At the end you will find writings on horticulture in Guernsey and a little on walking through around the Forest Parish, written by myself in 1997 for Guide Accreditation, for those who find this subject of interest for further reading.

Pre-War Years

The Circle of Life

I was born in June 1931, at a house known as 'Le Frie' in St. Pierre du Bois, Guernsey in the Channel Islands near France.

Apparently Father was overjoyed in having a son, as he'd had three daughters from a previous marriage. I was also named Frederick after him, my mother was Reta May, née Torode, of Les Padins in St. Saviour.

Whilst I obviously cannot remember anything of these earliest years, Mother told me that my father would often put me onto his shoulders to visit his mother who lived not far away at 'Les Vinaires'.

All was going well; in 1928 my father had bought a large field in La Route de Plaisance in the parish. It was two and a half miles from where we lived. Here, he built two glasshouses, 32 feet wide and 200 feet in length, heated by two large cast iron boilers. Tomatoes were grown and the fruit was then exported to England.

All was going so well, that Father decided to have a house built at the vinery. These glasshouses were known as vineries as the first greenhouses in the Island were used to grow grapes. The reason for having a house at the vinery meant that he and Mother no longer had to travel two and a half miles every day.

A design of house was chosen. The plot on which the house was to be built was marked out. All was going to plan, when tragedy struck. Father contracted tuberculosis; a cruel blow.

Father was confined to his bed. Mother now had to pick and pack the tomatoes on her own, although help was found.

The plans for building the house and further glasshouses were abandoned and in June 1933, Father died. He was only 64 and the last few months of his life were not pleasant.

Mother never told me anything about it but I overheard conversations she had with friends. I learned how painful his last few months were, Mother washing his back every day to ease the pain. The pain made him cry out and for many years after, the awful sounds I heard haunted me at night and sometimes even during the day.

I don't remember anything of the funeral. He was buried in the cemetery of the church of St. Pierre du Bois in the same place as his first wife.

I heard Mother say many times that the last words Father said were;

"Souogne au mousse"

"Look after the lad."

This she would do until her dying day, at the age of 86.

I have to admit that because of my misbehaviour and tantrums, looking after me was not easy. However, she never admonished me, nor gave me a severe 'ticking off'. In her eyes I could do no wrong. However, I can say without fear of contradiction that she carried out Father's instructions to the letter. Anyone else would likely have strangled me. Sadly, there were no photographs of my father; I have no idea what he looked like.

Grandmother and the New Hat

With Father's death, Mother now had to concentrate on me and the tomato business.

The four thousand plants had to be watered at least twice a week using a long and heavy hose. The plants had to be twisted up their strings and leaves removed, as the fruit ripened.

We moved to a new house in a Rue de La Madelaine; not that far away. We would visit my Grandmother from time to time; not that Mother wanted to but she felt that I should keep in touch. The tea we had was served in china cups with a pink brim. The cake that accompanied it was always slightly spiced.

On one visit; Mother had brought a new hat, which she was very proud of. After our tea, Mother said that she had to go to the lavatory, which was at a respectable distance from the house at the bottom of the garden. It was a narrow wooden structure, with a sloping roof and old fashioned red tiles.

It was euphemistically referred to as 'La petite maison' or 'the small house'. Inside there was a smooth wooden bench in which two round holes had been cut; one large for adults and the other small for children. Unfortunately, there was no flushing; everything simply fell in a deep hole.

As we approached the house, we heard my grandmother and aunt talking and laughing out loud. When we got nearer we heard my aunt say laughingly in Guernesiais, "Did you see her hat?! I wouldn't wear it to the lavatory!"

Mother charged in to confront them. She told them in strong language that we hadn't come to be ridiculed and we would never come again.

True to her word, we never did.

Looking After Us

We moved house once more, this time one and a half miles nearer to the vinery at La Rue des Prés. The house had been an old farmhouse built in granite, with a small wing attached; ideal for the two of us. The wing bordered a long narrow and winding lane, on one side there were meadows, hence the name – Road of Meadows.

It was very quiet in the lane; there were no motor vehicles. In the morning, farmers would lead their cows to the fields and return them to the farm in the evening. Sometimes cyclists would zip past, returning from a day's work and occasionally people would walk past; it was very quiet most of the time.

It was now the height of the season and although we now lived three quarters of a mile from the vinery, Mother had to spend most of the day there, except Sundays when we went to church.

Someone had to look after me; a person was found who lived in a farmhouse near the parish church. I hated it there. I spent most of the time alone in a stable that bordered on the lane. The bottom half of the door was closed, the top half open. All I could see was the sky.

One day I was crying and a lady passing heard me and looked in. As few people lived in the area, she knew who I was and told my mother what she had seen. When Mother called for me, she told the woman who was supposed to look after me what she thought of her. Thankfully, this meant I was spared any more hours of loneliness in that cold stable.

Instead, Mrs Brehaut, the lady living next door, offered to look after me. As it was school summer holidays, her children were at home and I was able to play with them. They would push my old pram with me in it, up and down the narrow lane. I was hanging on for dear life as we rounded bends at speed. Luckily, the lane was always free of traffic.

Later on towards the autumn, a man would visit us. I had no idea who he was. His son delivered him and picked him up as even though he owned a car, he couldn't drive. He was a widower; his name I later learned was Mr Ozanne. He was a tomato grower and a commission agent. He would find markets in England for growers, which he did for us.

I say us but, although I was unaware of it at the time, Norman Law that existed in Guernsey then meant that it was I who inherited the vinery and not my mother.

He also proved to be helpful in deterring my grandmother and uncles.

Although I didn't learn it until later, incredible though it is, on packing days my grandmother sent one of her sons to the vinery to count how many baskets of fruit were being exported and to make sure that they were all in my name. They thought that Mother was exporting some in her name, even though she would never have done such a thing.

Fortunately, on one packing day, Mr Ozanne visited us at the vinery. When one of my uncles arrived to count, Mr Ozanne was made aware for the reason of his visit. He threatened to take my uncle to the Royal Court if he ever returned. He never did.

The shed in which Mother packed tomatoes.

Another New Home

It was now the autumn of 1935 and the tomato crop was a great success, due mainly to the tremendous effort Mother had made. All bills were paid and there was sufficient money left to carry us through the winter.

We moved house once more, this time to one found for us by Mr Ozanne. It was in the next parish – the Forest – but only 200 yards from our vinery. This was going to make life easier for all of us.

The house was at the bottom of Farras Hill. Mr Ozanne lived at the top in a new bungalow, one hundred yards away. Because of the nearness of our two dwellings, his visits became more frequent.

I was delighted with the move as we now had a house on a main road, west from St. Peter Port. There was a lot more traffic than I had ever seen and buses passed near the house at regular intervals. It was a large semi-detached house and what pleased me most were the little conveniences; we had electricity in the house and we no longer had to fetch water from a well as we had a tap in the house with fresh water. To top it all, we had a toilet in the house that actually flushed into a cesspit.

With our new proximity, Mr Ozanne no longer needed his son to deliver him and on Sundays we would go for a drive in his car; very often to the north of the island where his son's fiancé lived.

I had never been to that part of the island before; it was like entering a new world. Unlike the valleys and cliffs we had, it was very much at sea-level and as flat as a pancake. I met two boys who lived near our vinery whose parents were tomato growers. We became good friends.

Life had changed for the better.

In Court

One day a letter arrived and its contents threatened our new found lifestyle. The letter was from the manager of Barclays Bank in St. Peter Po-t. He wanted Mother to go in for a chat.

I remember going with her; the bank was at the bottom of Fountain Street. We were shown into his office and he introduced himself as Mr Hill.

A problem had arisen because of the death of my father. He had borrowed money to pay for the glasshouses and the expensive boilers. The problem, as Mr. Hill explained, was that I had inherited the property and as I was a minor I couldn't be taken to court to recover the debt, which could have been recovered as vineries were going up in value. Everyone wanted a vinery and was prepared to pay above the odds. Hundreds of acres of glass were being built as investors knew that there were large profits to be made.

Mr Hill had noted how well Mother had done, so he was willing to allow her to continue to run the business on my behalf.

However, this could not be accepted by the bank without legal changes. If Mother became my legal guardian in law, she would be able to continue to run the business in my name but I would still be the owner. To achieve this, we had to go to the Royal Court.

I remember standing in front of the elderly Jurats and I was frightened as to what they were going to do to me. I needn't have worried; documents were signed and Mother was now my official guardian. The property was mine and no one could take it from me.

It was many years later that I learned that relatives of my father's side had tried to relieve me of the property. The attempt had failed, thanks to Mr Hill and the lawyers who had everything well under control.

A Mother's Work

The bank manager's faith in mother ability to run the business successfully was rewarded when our bank statement now showed that we were in credit.

At the end of the season, plants were removed from the glasshouses and the soil sterilised with chemicals. During the next five months there was no income, with long periods where there was little to do but unfortunately money was going out fast.

The soil had to be prepared, fertilisers applied and new tomato plants had to be purchased. They were planted into the soil in February, the boilers having been lit a few days before to warm the greenhouse. Tonnes of coal was brought and the boilers had to run day and night.

This was extremely expensive. During those few weeks with little to do, Mother found work on a farm in the area. Having been brought up on a farm, her experience was invaluable. I would go with her and enjoyed playing in the barns with the farmer's son as a companion.

Keeping the boilers burning day and night was the hardest job that Mother had to do. A very nice neighbour, Mr le Sauvage, also a grower, showed her how to light the fire, remove the clinkers and bank them at night. He came several times until Mother thanked him and said that she could now do it on her own.

Looking after the boilers was a hard and time consuming task. A five tonne load of anthracite coal was delivered and dumped alongside the boiler pit. The success of the crop relied on the boilers working efficiently at all times.

On arrival in the early morning, the first part of the vinery to be inspected was the boiler pit. If there was water in it, that had to be removed by bucket. Then coal had to be dropped into the pit. If some of the lumps were too large, they had to be reduced with a sledgehammer.

Mother would then descend into the pit which was five feet deep. Gloves had to be worn before the boiler door was opened. If the boiler had been working all night, the heat was intense. Mother had to step back to avoid being burnt by falling hot coals.

If there was still water in the pit it would cool the ashes and there would be great billows of steam, when this dispersed the fire could then be inspected. Sometimes there was a large clinker that covered the whole base of the boiler. The clinker had to be broken into smaller pieces to get it out, yet leaving as much of the fire in place as possible. It was an extremely skilled task that Mother had mastered. Coal was then shovelled into the boiler and the door closed. The ashes were raked out from under the boiler and put to one side. All this would be repeated with the other boiler opposite.

During the course of the day the boilers would be checked to see if more coal needed to be added. Towards dusk, the final task of the day, more coal was added; the ashes that had been moistened were shovelled on top of the coal to keep the fire burning until morning. Mother undertook this arduous task every day from early February to late June.

This she did without complaint for six consecutive years. The success of our tomato growing business could be put down to her skill, hard work and dedication

She was admired by all growers in the area for what she had achieved. It was agreed without exception, that no man could have done better.

Hard Labours Bear Fruit

The most rewarding part of the tomato season began in early May. There were bunches of fruit on each plant at regular intervals. The fruit was swelling. Then the result of Mother's hard work – a ripe tomato, soon followed by lots more.

They were picked three times a week before being graded and tipped into wooden baskets which were lined with different coloured paper that indicated the grade. The lids were nailed down and labels with the name of a town were stapled into the side. An invoice sheet was filled in for each salesman and Mr Ozanne's lorry would collect the baskets and deliver them to the harbour. Only then came the long awaited cheques that were taken to the bank.

This was the first time money was coming in since October last. There was finally money to spend but only on what was absolutely necessary; none was wasted. If something not vital was needed, Mother would say "We'll get it when we can afford it."

At least once a week, we'd go to the Forest Post Office that doubled up as a grocery shop. It belonged to Mrs. De Beauchamp, a short elderly lady. The shop was no more than a small wooden shed and the interior was poorly lit, even more so in winter when the only form of lighting was a large oil lamp suspended from the ceiling.

It could only take a few customers at a time, so when there were lots a queue formed in the lane. Fortunately, the road was seldom used by most motor vehicles. Patience was needed and the parish gossip was passed around.

The highlight of these trips for me was when, as a treat, we would buy a large coconut cake with a cherry on top, made by Lyons.

Health

Mother was always very careful how money was spent, however, there were times when she never hesitated to spend some. One of these was on my health.

Every time I had a nasty cough or she thought I was going to have a cold, I would be taken to see the doctor.

The surgery was at Le Longfrie, in a large and very old house built in grey Guernsey granite. We would enter through a large and heavy door that led into a dimly lit corridor. There was a line of chairs in varying shapes and sizes on which patients sat and waited to be called by the doctor.

There were no appointments, people simply turned up. It was a first come first served system. There were times when people were unsure whose turn it was and invariably while they were working it out, Mother would grab hold of my arm and drag me quickly into the doctor's room. It was always either old Mr Bisson, or his son, always referred to as young Mr Bisson. I preferred the young one but more often than not I would be seen by his father.

The reason for my many trips to the doctor was because Mother didn't want me to suffer the pain and agony that Father had endured for so long. It might seem that these visits were unnecessary but when I was nineteen years of age, a friend wanted to sell me Life Insurance and I found out something interesting.

I filled in a form for him and a question asked 'What was the cause of your father's death?' I answered honestly and because of this they would not accept me unless I received a full examination. I agreed and an appointment was made for me to see Dr Cambridge at his surgery in the High Street, St. Peter Port.

His examination was thorough and when he finished he told me all was well, although when I was a small boy I had at some point contacted Tuberculosis. It had been cured and wouldn't cause me further problems, and I was accepted for the insurance.

This was sixty seven years ago! All those visits to the Doctor had paid off.

A Near Miss

I was soon old enough not to require a minder whilst Mother was working. Having moved to the Forest Parish, I met two boys who lived near us, they were David and Ken. Their parents were growers too and we spent a lot of time together.

La Route de Plaisance that passed our vinery was a major road leading to the West Coast. It was a bus route and there were a few motor cars. One day I was at David's house and stayed too long, when Mother was expecting me for tea. I dashed out of their gate to reach the footpath on the other side. I hadn't checked to see if the road was clear of traffic and hadn't seen a car approaching from the east.

Fortunately, the car wasn't going that fast, the driver slammed on his brakes and the car stopped inches from my legs. I, however, didn't stop. I ran the hundred yards along the pavement until I reached home. I flung open the back door, raced in and slumped into the chaise longue; my heart pounding at an unhealthy rate.

Before Mother could see me, there was a knock at the back door; it was the driver who had miraculously saved my life. He reported to her what had happened, sounding very upset. Mother thanked him and assured him that I was unharmed. It was a great relief to the man and he calmed down but advised Mother to reiterate to me about waiting until the road is safe to cross.

School & New Language

Once you reached the age of five, you had to go to school. The Forest Parish School was no more than a quarter of a mile away and Mother walked me there. It was a new experience for me but I soon settled into the routine.

The language most spoken in the South West was the Norman French; Le Guernesiais, sometimes it is referred to as 'Patois'. I was brought up with it as all our neighbours and relatives spoke it and Mother and I only spoke Guernesiais when we were together.

On returning home from my first day at school Mother asked me what I had done that day, to which I replied I was learning a foreign language.

"They call it English," I told her.

After a year there, Mother realised that I wasn't making sufficient progress in the new language and something had to be done. Money that had been set aside could now be used for something necessary. After some research, a place was found for me at the States of Guernsey Intermediate School for Girls, in St. Peter Port. The school had three classrooms in the east wing for young children until the age of eight; boys were also allowed in this age range if you paid.

I enjoyed my stay there even though it was rather posh. I learned how to read and write in English. No Guernesiais was spoken there and my command of the English language improved rapidly because of it.

We learned all sorts of things. I remember making bags out of raffia and lining the inside with coloured material. We also had music lessons with drums, recorders and other instruments. Unfortunately I was always given a triangle and there is not a lot one can do with that! I used to strike it more than I should even though it never failed to get me reprimanded.

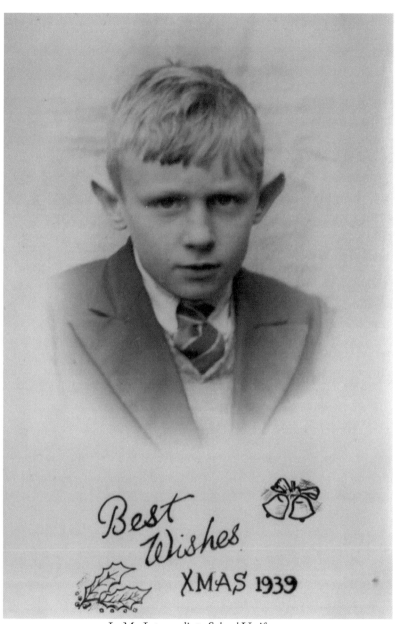

In My Intermediate School Uniform

The Bus

As the school was four and a half miles from home, I had to catch a bus. It was red and cream and belonged to the Guernsey Bus Company.

There were no official bus stops in those days. I waited on the footpath outside our gate and the bus stopped when the driver saw me. Occasionally, I wasn't there in time and the bus still stopped and the driver – Harold Gallienne, not related– would blow the horn very hard. It never took very long for me to appear, dragged by my mother. As I ran to the other side of the bus to climb in, Harold and Mother would exchange pleasantries in Guernesiais. Even with these delays, Harold would always deliver us at the top of the Grange in time for us to walk the last quarter mile to school.

During the season Mother would nip to the vinery early, to check if everything was all right, open the ventilators and check the boilers. She would then return to get me ready for school.

On one occasion there must have been a problem that had to be rectified and she was late coming home. There was no way that I would be ready for the bus – It arrived, stopped and the hooter was blown. Mother rushed to tell Harold not to wait; it would be a while before I was ready. Reluctantly, but to the relief of the passengers, he moved on.

So far, I had never missed a day at school and Mother didn't want me to miss one now. When I was ready, she fished out her old bicycle; a 1920s model, with no gears.

I was instructed to jump on the back and we set off up the steep Farras Hill. The seat was metal and was very hard and uncomfortable as I held on for dear life with my legs clinging on either side of the rear wheel. We eventually reached the top of the hill, leaving only four and a half miles to go! Fortunately, after Farras, the road is either flat or down hill into Town.

With a quarter of a mile yet to go, we stopped at a small shop. I was glad of a rest from the hard seat. To my great delight I was given some chocolate, as I had not had breakfast. I was ordered to finish it before I reached school.

One we reached school we went to my classroom where Mother apologised for my late arrival, which my teacher accepted graciously. Mother then had to cycle home, fortunately without me on the back, as it was almost all uphill until home.

Grapes & Downtime.

Sometimes, there was little to do in the glasshouses, so Mother would help a farmer who had glasshouses with grapes that needed to be thinned - a specialist job. The glasshouses were usually 38 feet wide and the vines would stretch from the low side to the apex. In order to reach the grapes, a simple staircase was made. Up to six women would sit two abreast. They had very pointed scissors to prune the grapes; everything small would be removed and they would also make sure the bunches of grapes had a good shape. Once the first section was finished, the staircase was moved sideways.

It was a most boring task, so there was continuous chatter and gossiping. I wouldn't stay as I felt the gossip was not for my ears. I would play in the barns and on the old fashioned machinery.

On Sundays, in the summer when the fires were out, we would visit relatives. Mother's brother lived at Les Padins, bordering the reservoir. It was two miles away and we went on foot.

At 5:15pm we left our relatives and walked the two and a half miles to the Forest Methodist Church, where my stepfather-to-be was a trustee and took the collection. After the service, the three of us went for a walk at Le Bourg. We would descend the lane leading to Petit Bôt Bay, then through the lanes to Stepfather's house for tea. It took ages as we met several people we knew and they would chat for what seemed like forever.

At the top of the road leading down to Petit Bôt, there was a shop. It was closed at that sort of time but outside there was a box and if I fed three one penny coins into it, a bar of chocolate would fall out. On one of these occasions, I had a six pence piece and planned to get two bars. I fed in the coin, pressed the button... but nothing happened! No two bars of chocolate!

When I mentioned this to a friend, he laughed and explained that the machine worked only with pennies. He suggested that I go to the shop, explain what I had done and ask for my six pence. I never went, though... I didn't want them to see what a stupid idiot I had been!

Another New School

Time was moving on and I was approaching eight years of age, my time at the school for girls was coming to an end, as boys had to leave at that age. At that time, I thought the reason boys had to leave was because older boys might have a disruptive influence on the girls. However, many years later I met a woman who had been a teacher there and she told me that my assumption was incorrect. She maintained that the boys were asked to leave purely and simply for their own safety, as some of the girls over eight can become vicious and aggressive towards boys of that age. Although I believed her at the time, later I came to the conclusion that she was having a joke at my expense!

I reached the age of eight in June, so a new school had to be found for me in September. Some boys would go on to Elizabeth College but most would go to the States of Guernsey Intermediate School for Boys which was only two hundred yards from the girl's one.

I didn't want to go back to a parish school and my preferred school was Elizabeth College. They had the best sports ground in the island and I wanted to be a part of it!

Money, of course, was the problem; the fees at that school were very high. The tomato season wasn't over and Mother had to wait to see to which school she could afford to send me.

It was decided after much deliberation, that I should go to the States of Guernsey School for Boys. Not a bad choice; it was a top class Grammar School. She had really wanted me to go to Elizabeth College but she had always been one not to spend what she couldn't afford. She disliked borrowing and even worse she hated being in debt. She consoled me by saying if all goes well, I could go to the college next year.

I was accepted into the Grammar School and a uniform had to be bought. This was a black blazer and grey trousers. The school tie was in the colours of the States; green and black in equal amount and separated by a thin white line. The cap was black with an upturned 'V' in front which bore the colour of your school house. My house was Mesny and its colour was yellow.

Every morning before lessons began, we all assembled outdoors in our houses for inspection. Improperly dressed and dirty shoes were not tolerated. I can still vividly recall our teacher, Miss Jones. She was a short plump woman in middle age who wore large glasses and had protruding front teeth. She spoke with an accent that I did not recognise.

I settled into my new school quite well and soon we all began to learn French.

My Bicycle.

Mother decided to buy me a bicycle without gears in order to get to school. I had not long reached my eighth birthday and wasn't too keen to cycle the 4 and half miles to Town on my own and put in my objections. Mother simply countered this by telling me that it would do me good, as well as saving us money.

Cycling to school in the autumn of 1939 was quite good and dry. I cycled down to town fairly easily and on the way home some boys accompanied me for part of the way. However when winter arrived, the daylight hours became short, the weather colder and it rained. If it was raining, my mother decided I could use the bus as it was safer. However if it was dry in the morning I was to use my bike.

One morning the weather was fine enough for me to cycle and in the afternoon, when I left school, it was still dry even though there were rumblings overhead. Unfortunately I had gone about half a mile when the heavens opened and the rain pelted down. I stopped and sheltered under a tree. Lightning flashed overhead and I decided it was unsafe to continue sheltering, so I cycled on. It was getting dark rapidly and I had no lights on the bike.

By the time I got home I was drenched and sneezing. Mother was horrified when she saw the state of me; all the advice that old Dr Bisson had given her had been forgotten and she had visions of my ending up like Father. My wet clothes were removed and my body dried thoroughly with a towel. I put on clothes that had been warmed near the fire and was given a tot of Brandy, which Mother kept for medicinal purposes only. Then it was up to bed with a hot water bottle.

The next morning, I was taken to Le Longfrie Surgery. When young Dr Bisson learned what had happened he told Mother in no uncertain terms that the bicycle must be put aside for the rest of the winter and I must take the bus.

Money Troubles

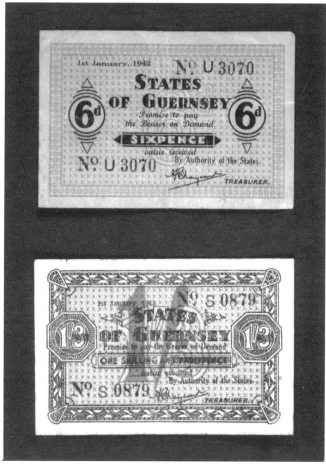

Guernsey banknotes issued during the Occupation
© *Guernsey Museums & Galleries*

I enjoyed going to school by bus and Mother always gave me six pence; three pence to go, three pence to return. I never needed any more as I always took a packed lunch that was quite sufficient. One day, I saw boys going to the tuck shop and they were buying a tub made of wafer, filled with marshmallow and topped with chocolate. They looked delicious! This time I couldn't resist, so I bought one with the bus money.

It truly was delicious but then it hit me; I had spent my bus fare. I was faced with a four and a half mile walk home that was mainly uphill. As I left school, I braced myself and consoled myself that it wasn't going to be too difficult! At the top of the Grange lots of boys and girls were waiting for their bus. I walked past quickly.

After a couple of miles I felt tired, mainly due to the hills. I soldiered on and reached the Forest Road, which is about a mile long but luckily mostly flat. At the end is Le Chêne Hill and it is steep – I managed to get to the top with a massive effort. I needed a rest and sat for a while on a low ledge. After that it was thankfully downhill, so I moved on to Le Bourg and the sharp right-hand hill that reaches the entrance to the airport. I took a deep breath and told myself that there was only one mile left.

I had only moved a few yards when Mother appeared on her old bicycle. She applied the brakes suddenly enough that they protested with a screeching noise. She was so relieved to see me that she didn't even ask why I was walking. I was ordered to get on her bike and we reached home in record time – I then had to explain why I wasn't on the bus. I was going to say that I had lost my bus fare, but decided to tell the truth. Except when asked why I had done that, I lied and said that it was because I was hungry. This was of course untrue; the reason I had spent the money was pure greed! However, I did gain something from this incident; to avoid it happening again, I was given pocket money.

Quite often after school I would walk into the centre of town with other boys; sometimes I bought a comic, usually *Film Fun*, and sometimes a bar of chocolate. Then I would catch the bus at the station or the top of the Grange. In those days our bus reached the Grange via the long steep hill of Victoria Road; it was especially hard going along the last fifty yards. Sometimes, some of us would dash down those fifty yards to meet the bus as it was always struggling by then with its small engine protesting loudly. Our aim was to race the bus to the top, fortunately we always won.

Image courtesy of John Carman 'A History of Guernsey Buses, Coaches & Trains'

Sundays

I spent a lot of time with my new friends, David and Ken, other than Sunday; which was a day of rest and for going to church.

One Sunday I shall never forget, Mother said that she needed to visit the vinery to check something, telling me to stay indoors as she wouldn't be long. Obediently, I stayed in the dining room and played with the few toys I had. She was away longer than usual and to begin with I wasn't worried; I thought she might have met a neighbour and stopped to chat.

Time ticked away on our old Grandfather clock and I began to be worried, so I went upstairs to our bedroom. It had a small window in the gable-side facing west. I sat on the window seat as from there I would see Mother returning.

I waited and waited but she didn't come. Now I was very worried... had she fallen into the boiler pit? What if she had hurt herself and couldn't get out? I didn't know what to do. I wondered if I should go to our neighbour Mrs Crawshaw and tell her Mother hadn't come home.

I decided to take one final look and it was with enormous relief that I saw Mother rounding the corner. I slid off the window seat and ran down the stairs and began to play with my toys as if I had never been worried but as she entered, I ran and hugged her.

She apologised for taking longer than planned and I never told her how long I had looked for her from the bedroom window.

On this particular Sunday we were due to visit Mother's brother and family who lived two and a half miles away in St. Saviours. Other Sundays we would visit her sister Elise who lived around the corner. We always had to make sure we left in time to reach the Forest Methodist Church in time for service.

The other services Mother enjoyed very much were the ones at small chapels, usually at Easter, where children from their Sunday Schools recited short passages from the Bible. This service was known as 'L'Anniversaire'.

One of these services in particular will remain with me forever. It took place at a very small chapel named 'Le Douit d'Israel', where young children were doing their recitations. I marvelled at how cool they were because when I had to learn short passages at my Sunday School, I froze. I couldn't get a word out. One of the teachers would always end up rescuing me and escorting me away.

When the children had finished, there was silence. The minister stood up and it appeared that he was looking at me, when he announced in

Guernesiais, that Frederick Gallienne was going to sing! I was appalled; I hadn't even been asked! There was silence in the chapel and heads began to look in my direction. Fortunately, I was sat along the aisle, so I looked towards the exit that wasn't far away. I stood and was about to sprint outside when a man who had been sat a few rows ahead of me, stood up and began to sing. I sat down again, slowly, my heart beating at an unhealthily fast rate.

By the end of the service, it had slowed down and when we were outside, I told Mother that I didn't want to come here again! We never did but still every time I pass that building, my heart misses a few beats.

Rat Catching

I was always delighted when Monday arrived and I could resume playing with my friends. One day I caught up with them and they said that they were going down the road to the shop owned by two elderly spinsters, whose surname was James, to buy some sweets. They invited me along but I had no money. I asked Mother who was busy in the glasshouse but she had none with her either.

I wasn't going to give up though and an idea came to me; something that I'd used before. I went to see our friendly neighbours and I asked them if they had any dead rats, no luck at first, then one said that there should be a rat in one of their traps by the shed. There was one, so he removed the dead rat from the trap and took it into his shed and with a chopper he chopped off its tail, then wrapped it in brown paper.

He knew I was going to the shop; I now had to change the tail into hard cash.

We lived in the Forest Parish and our vinery was in the parish of St. Pierre du Bois. I should have gone to a constable of one of these but this would have meant going away from the shop. The Constable of the parish of St. Saviour, Mr Vidamour, lived much nearer.

I ran through the fields to his farm and luckily he was in the house. When he answered the door, he saw the brown paper with the end of a tail visible and knew what I wanted. He had the right to refuse but as Mother was one of his best grape-thinners, he thought it best to pay me the three pence that was the reward for catching a rat. He also knew that if he had refused, Mother would be knocking on his door inquiring whey he hadn't paid me. So he went indoors to his desk, unlocked a small tin box from which he produced three pennies and noted the transaction in a book.

I sprinted away and met the others returning from the shop, sucking their chosen sweets. The shop was closing in five minutes and as I climbed the steps to the shop, one Miss James was approaching the door with the key.

I quickly bought a chocolate Milky Way for one penny. It had a card on top with a picture of stars on it. I spent the remaining two pence on hard toffees, which she put into a white paper cone-shaped bag. I felt it sensible to choose toffees over boiled sweets because they lasted longer.

My Mother's Story

There were two occupations that Mother wanted for me. One was to be a bank manager and the other to be an organist at the parish church. She felt that these two professions were the height of respectability. She also wanted me to have a life of minimum effort, unlike hers.

Mother was brought up on a farm, where children were an asset. She had three brothers and three sisters and all were expected to do their share of the work. Her father, by all accounts, was a strict disciplinarian. Mother was the sixth born but her older siblings saw to it that there was no slacking on her part. Before going to school, there were cows to milk and after that she would climb the steep hill to St. Saviours School. On her return it was back to work.

Her mother too, was expected to work like a slave and walk once a week to town; four and a half miles and back.

Mother knew roughly when her mother would return. She would always run through the narrow lanes to meet her, hoping that there were sweets for her. Her other two sisters didn't enjoy the life that they were forced to lead. At the first opportunity, they married. Mother had left school by then and was now a full-time worker on the farm and because of her sisters' departure, there was definitely more work to do.

It was a hard and lonely life as few people ventured down the winding lanes. The only time she met strangers was on a Sunday, when she went to her parish church. Because her family were land owners they had their own pew. Mother related many times to me how embarrassed she was when there were people occupying theirs and her father would go into a rage; waving his walking stick over his head menacingly, forcing them to vacate their family's pew.

After her mother died, things got even lonelier and it took her a long time to recover. Then something happened that changed her life dramatically; her father died. This meant a complete change of ownership. As Norman Law stood in Guernsey, the eldest son inherited the farm but his siblings received nothing.

Unlike today, farms then were small but a most important business. If all the children received an equal share, none would be able to earn a living. Having only one owner, the farm would survive. Mother was now left homeless and with no money. She heard from a friend that a family in Reading, in England, were looking for a housekeeper, so she applied and was accepted. Mother recounted on many occasions that this had been a bad move, as she was back in the world of slavery.

However, as soon as she had saved enough money, she left and came home to Guernsey. Once home, another farmer relative took her in and once again her life was about to change; this time for the better. She met a man, who later became my father. I have no details of how they met, but he was a widower, his wife had died a few years earlier and even though he was many years older than Mother, they married.

Father was an established tomato grower, which he had achieved by hard work and business sense. Not being the eldest son, when his father died he did not inherit the farm and did not receive any money.

Mother was now involved with a completely different form of work. No longer involved with farming, she was pleased with the change that the industry of growing provided. She loved animals and she had always cried when they were sent for slaughter.

Tomato growing was now big business; Father had plans to double the size of the vinery. Mother took to her new way of life with great enthusiasm; it was more enjoyable as she was working with someone on equal terms. The work was less physical than before, yet she still wanted me to have a lifestyle even less arduous.

Piano

In 1939, Mother read in the local newspaper that a man living in the Torteval Parish had a harmonium for sale. We went to see it and found it in the living room of an old farmhouse. Mother liked it and immediately began negotiations for a price that satisfied both parties. The farmer was happy with the transaction - so much so, that he volunteered to deliver it by horse and cart, without charge.

Mother lost no time in finding someone to teach me to play it. He lived nearby and I went to his house. His harmonium was of a much better quality than mine and easier to play. I think that Mother's powers of persuasion left the young man with no alternative but to take me on. After a while, he gathered enough courage to tell her that unfortunately, due to other commitments, he was unable to continue with my lessons.

It didn't take Mother long to find another teacher, a young woman whose name was Peggy. I had to cycle to her home known as Chertsy House, near what is now Carlton Hotel. She had a piano which I found easier to play as it had no pedals to pump. I learned about quavers, semibreves and such and was given pieces of music to practice at home.

This wasn't easy as the harmonium was old and the stiff pedals had to be worked by foot. I found it extremely difficult to concentrate on the music while peddling at the same time. I told Mother that I wished that she had bought me a piano. She explained that churches had organs, so I had to persevere.

One day I complained bitterly that I couldn't concentrate on the music and work the pedals at the same time. Mother, who always wanted to be helpful, got down on her knees and began to work the pedals with the palm of her hands. This made a massive difference but unfortunately, even though Mother was very strong physically, with the stiff pedals she couldn't keep it up during the whole of my practice session.

Locally Famous...

Unfortunately, it was not my musical talents which got me noticed locally but rather my unlucky experience at the vinery.

We had new neighbours with children; one boy was about my age but wasn't popular with any of my friends. He arrived at our vinery one day and said that he wanted to play. I apologised and told him that my mother and I were going out shortly. He didn't take that too well and as we passed the boiler pit, without warning, he pushed me into it.

It was February and the pit had about a few feet of water in the bottom. Fortunately, Mother had hired a man to help prepare the soil for planting, a Mr Ozanne; he heard the splash, rushed out and heard my pleas for help. Quickly, he rescued me from the foul water. By this point, Mother had rushed out of the shed to see what was going on. She was appalled with what had happened, wanting to know how I came to be in the pit.

To make matters worse, I was wearing wellington boots and they were full of filthy water. We emptied these but as we walked home my feet made a slushy noise. I had no idea how much water I had swallowed.

The following day, the local newspaper carried a report of the embarrassing incident. Mr Ozanne was hailed a hero for his rescue. The perpetrator never came near me again. I believe Mother had a not too quiet word in his mother's ear.

The Army

One day, as I was walking down the lane I saw someone ascending Farras Hill.

As he got closer, I recognised him as a neighbour; he was wearing a khaki uniform. He had volunteered to join the British Army, to 'teach those Jerries a lesson'.

His mother was shocked when she learned what he had done. She told Mother that she still hadn't fully recovered from losing a brother in the Great War. I wished him luck, although little did I know that I wouldn't see another soldier in that uniform for five years!

On our way to school in St. Peter Port, we had gotten used to seeing two soldiers of the Royal Irish Fusiliers on sentry duty at the entrance to the residence of the Lieutenant Governor. Somehow it always gave us a sense of security. When the regiment went to France in 1939, we all felt uneasy.

However, not all news was bad. Mother told me that in early 1940 she was negotiating for me to go to Elizabeth College in September. At last my wish was to be fulfilled but soon after this marvellous news, my life was to be turned upside down.

An unpleasant man by the name of Herr Hitler had decided to begin a war.

For a while, not a lot happened, and it began to be known as 'The Phoney War'. However, in the spring of 1940, Hitler made moves to invade territories in Europe; his troops were heading our way. There was nervousness in the air; surely he wasn't coming this far?

On arriving at school one morning, we were told that we were going to St. George's Hall in the town. This large hall was filled with children from many schools. We were told about the situation and that Hitler wasn't a nice person.

We sang patriotic songs, such as *Land of Hope and Glory*, and many others, ending with *God Save the King* in full voice.

Soon after, schools were closed. There was a great deal of uncertainty around; it looked as though our small island would be sucked into the war.

After Dunkirk, the German forces advanced rapidly through Europe and there was talk of Hitler landing in the Channel Islands. Our Government had sent a large sum of money to the British Government to help with the war effort and to defend us. This they failed to do; the most they did was to evacuate those who wished to leave, including the children.

Children of school age had priority, if their families decided to send them; they would assemble at a prominent place and be taken by bus to the harbour. Able-bodied men left and many volunteered to join the British Forces. Adults and babies made their way to the harbour and had to wait for long hours for a boat to arrive. If they were lucky enough to find one, it would be more than a fourteen-hour journey to England.

As the Germans approached the Cherbourg peninsular, boats were few and far between. One family walked four miles to the harbour, four times. They waited hours on each occasion and no boats arrived. In the end they decided to remain on the island and take their chances. No one knows exactly how many islanders got away; some figures say it was in the region of 21,000, which meant that 19,000 of us remained. How so many people managed to get away without their boats being sunk by German U-boats is, I believe, a miracle.

Many more people would have evacuated had they been able. Mother was undecided what to do with me; to send me away or keep me close? Sometimes she would cry, not knowing what would be best for me. One morning, very early, she entered my bedroom and told me that she had heard on the wireless that a ship leaving the port of Liverpool with

British children aboard had been sunk. This terrible news had helped her make up her mind. I was staying with her.

As schools were closed, I had plenty of time on my hands. I wandered around the Forest Parish to see how many of my friends remained. The sum total was none! For the first time in my life I felt lonely and abandoned. I knocked on many doors, some locked but most unlocked. These I entered but there was not a sound from within. The dining room tables had items on them, all the things you would expect for breakfast. It was frightening; cups half filled with cold tea, cereals hardly touched and mouldy. Entire families had fled, not bothering to clear away the dishes as if they expected never to return to them.

Day followed by miserable day. No change, no one to be seen; a more depressing state of affairs could not be imagined for a child. At least some families had their domestic pets put down humanely. Others did not bother and simply abandoned them, leaving them to survive as best they could. I too, felt abandoned... was I going to grow up surrounded only by elderly adults and babes in arms? Surely this could not be?! Heaven forbid!

Worse still, our local shop had run out of sweets, which surprised me as there was an acute shortage of children. Oh, why hadn't I left with my school? I was certain my form mates were having a marvellous time in England. Was I ever going to get to Elizabeth College? I had my doubts. What was going to happen to our island and to us?

The Occupation

A Bit of Background...

The islands of Guernsey, Alderney, Sark and Herm became part of the Duchy of Normandy in about 900 AD

In 1066, William the Conqueror, the then Duke of Normandy, also became King of England but in 1204 King John lost control of Normandy.

This posed my ancestors and others a problem; did we go with France or remain loyal to the English crown? French was the official language of the island, so going with the French would be easy, however the most spoken language was the Norman of William the Conqueror so we decided to remain loyal to our Duke.

With the loss of Normandy, the islands now had to be protected from the French and so from then on castles and forts were built and a military presence defended us until 1939.

Having such a mighty power to protect us, the people of these islands felt safe and secure but things were about to change and threaten this cosy existence.

On the 3rd September of that year, Great Britain declared war on Germany. The British garrison in Guernsey left in late 1939 to join up with the British forces in France and in January 1940 the Royal Guernsey Militia was disbanded.

For the first time in 800 years, Guernsey was left with no defence.

So it was that this island with its 40,000 inhabitants could only look on with some trepidation at the speed the German Forces were making towards our shores.

Whitehall now believed that the strategic importance of the islands had been reduced.

Incredibly the British Government were unaware of their responsibility for our defence.

Perhaps it was thought that as the islands were no longer of strategic importance, that the Germans would not need them either.

However, should the Germans take over, they would have to be removed as a matter of prestige.

The Violent Beginning of the Occupation

In June 1940, it was suggested that the Foreign Office should inform the Germans that we were undefended; whilst this could be an invitation for the enemy to walk in it might save the people from aerial bombing. This idea was later abandoned.

Instead, the British Government decided that evacuating the people was all they could do, starting with school children and men of military age.

Around half the population of the island was evacuated, with more waiting to go but unable to as the Germans had gotten too close.

For some time the German forces kept an eye on the island as they could not believe that it would be undefended. On 28th June 1940 a German plane was flying over when they viewed what the thought was a line of military vehicles at the harbour and attacked with bombs and machinegun fire.

The unfortunate truth of the matter was that these were merely lorries laden with tomatoes for export, covered with tarpaulins to protect the fruit from the hot sun.

Many of the 33 men who died had hidden under the vehicles to protect themselves but died as the lorries collapsed on top of them, leaving another 80 with injuries.

Mother and I lived five miles from the harbour and could hear the bombardment, although as yet unaware of the carnage that had taken place.

The remains of tomato lorries at White Rock, St Peter Port after a bombing raid by the German Luftwaffe on Thursday 28th June, 1940
© Guernsey Museums & Galleries

Within a couple of days the British announced both news of the bombing and the fact that Guernsey had been demilitarised.

It comes as no surprise that soon after the planes of the Luftwaffe flew over the airport, having learned that the island was undefended.

As we lived close to the airport, and knowing what had happened at the harbour, my mother suggested we go to the bottom of our lane and hide under the trees.

The plane circled warily to check for any signs of resistance before landing whilst another two continued circling overhead just in case.

It seemed mere moments until a German officer appeared with a revolver in hand, accompanied by three or four other soldiers with rifles.

A neighbour left his home to confront the Germans and my mother pulled us out of hiding to go and see what they wanted, seeing as they were not about to bomb us.

The officer spoke excellent English and wanted to know the distance to the nearest telephone exchange, to which our neighbour told him it was three miles. It was then that they noticed our car; a Hillman that had not yet been run in.

Without so much as an ask, he ordered his men to get it and we could only watch as our car disappeared down the road, not realising that we wouldn't see it again for five years.

That was my introduction to the occupation of our island, as German soldiers soon flooded in through the harbour for a stay that would not be a short one.

Settling in

In no time at all the Germans began to quickly build anti-aircraft positions around the airport out of wood, using soil to keep the wood in place.

One of these was positioned only two fields away from our vinery and as we could no longer export our tomatoes, my mother asked me to take a basketful and some cucumbers to see if they would buy them.

The ack-ack gun was in centre of the emplacement and there were six soldiers with helmets around it ready to fire should they need, whilst a few others were lounging on the ground relaxing.

They smiled when they saw me but when I asked if they wanted to buy the produce they didn't understand. Just as I was about to leave a soldier in field grey uniform come out of the wooden hut and asked in passable English what I wanted.

2cm FLAK.38 Anti-Aircraft Position in wooden emplacement in St Andrew's,
Image from Festung Guernsey
© *Guernsey Museums & Galleries*

Once I told him, he took the basket and gave me a note to the value of 50 pfennigs.

I ran back to the vinery quite happy with the transaction, not knowing what it was worth.

However we were terribly disappointed, upon taking it to the Forest Post Office, to discover that it was worth no more than one shilling and one penny. Mother was furious and refused to offer them anymore.

Soon notices began to appear in the Guernsey Press, informing us what we could and could not do. This was directed at adults and at only nine years old I was told only what I needed to know... such as curfew.

We couldn't leave the house before 8am and had to be back inside by 10pm. Anyone found outside of those hours could be shot, as impressed upon me by my Mother when on one occasion I stayed out past 10pm.

Identity cards were issued to adults and my name was added to my mother's as I was under fourteen.

REGISTRATION FORM.

Two copies of this Form must be completed by every person. If you are in doubt as to how to complete this Form, the Constable or a Douzenier of your Parish will help you.

For Official use only.

No.

(a) Surname in block letters followed by Christian names. (a) *GALLIENNE* *RETA. MAY*

(b) Ordinary Postal address, including Parish (b) *Farras* *Forest*

(c) Date of Birth (c) *April 16* *1900*

(d) Place of Birth (d) *Les Paclin* *S Saviours* *GUERSEY*

(e) Nationality* (e) *British*

(f) Occupation (f) *Greenhouse* *work.*

(g) Single, married, widow or widower (g) *Widow*

(h) Colour of hair (h) *Brown*

(i) Colour of eyes (i) *Blue*

(j) Any physical peculiarities, such as a scar, limp, etc. (j)

(k) Have you served in any of His Britannic Majesty's Armed Forces ? If so, write R.N., R.N.R., Army, B.A.F., Royal Guernsey Militia, or as is appropriate and give your rank on retirement and the date of retirement (k)

(l) Are you on a Reserve of Officers of His Britannic Majesty's Armed Forces ? If so, state which Reserve (l)

(m) Are you, not being on a Reserve of Officers, on the Reserve of any of His Britannic Majesty's Armed Forces ? If so, state which Reserve. (m)

*As regards question (e), if you are a person possessing dual nationality, give both nationalities.

	RELATIONSHIP	NAME	RANK	BRANCH OF SERVICE
(n) Have you a husband, son, grandson, brother, father, nephew, uncle, or first cousin actually serving in any of His Britannic Majesty's Armed Forces ? If so, give his relationship to you and his full name and rank and state which branch (such as R.N., Army, R.A.F., or as the case may require) of the Forces he belongs to. Do not give his Unit or any particulars of his last known whereabouts.				

If this space for your answer is insufficient, complete your answer on the reverse of

	RELATIONSHIP	NAME
(o) Have you a husband, son, grandson, brother, father, nephew, uncle or first cousin who is, to your knowledge, on a Reserve of Officers of His Britannic Majesty's Armed Forces ? If so, give his relationship to you and his full name and address.		

(p) Having completed the answers to the above questions (and where the answer to any of the word "No" must be written) take this Form to a Constable or Douzenier of your Parish (in take it to the Seneschal) and write your usual signature in his presence and add the date.

(Signature) *R. M. Gallienne*

(Date) *29. 1940*

Your signature must be witnessed by the Official before whom it is signed and he will sign his name and add his official title and the name of the Parish of which he is an Official.

Witnessed by

(Signature)

(Title)

(Name of Parish)

Identity Card issued by (Official issuing Identity Card to insert his initials.)

STAR TYP., BORDAGE—60M/10/1940.

Front of Mother's Occupation ID Form.
(Courtesy of the Island Archives)

(a) 1 Surname in Block letters **GALLIENNE. NEE FORODE** st of Identity Card **2329**

2 Christian Names **RETA. MAY.** **WIDOW**

3 Present address **RUE PERROT** **FOREST**

4 Date of birth **APRIL 16. 1900**

5 Place of birth (Country or Island) **GUERNSEY**

6 Occupation **HOUSEWORK**

7 Place of Employment **NORMANHURST FOREST**

8 Name of Employer **GERMAN AUTHORITIES.**

(b) 9. Date of commencement of residence in Channel Islands

FULL NAME	No. of Identity Card	Date of Birth	Place of Birth (Country or Island)
(c) Of Wife (if now in Channel Islands)			
(d) Of all children, including adopted children (of whatever age they may be) forming part of the declarant's household.			
FREDDIE. GALLIENNE		**JUNE 26ᵗʰ 1931**	**GUERNSEY**

Date **Dec 23ʳᵈ 1942.** Signature **Reta May Gallienne**

NAME of **CHILD**. **PLACE + DATE of BIRTH** **FATHER'S NAME.**
Freddie Gallienne. **Milton, Les Manes, St Peters** **Frederick Gallienne.**
26 - 6 - 1931.

ADDRESS of CHILD **Is THE FATHER LIVING IN GUERNSEY?**
Farras Forest **Deceased**

Back of Mother's Occupation ID Form, showing my name added on.
(Courtesy of the Island Archives)

Moving

As more soldiers arrived, they needed accommodation.

Our invaders were very cunning and, as half the population had gone, there were many empty houses which were quickly taken up by them. It was just as well that the owners now in England and Scotland had no idea that their precious possessions were being used by the enemy.

This practice saved the Germans a lot of money as they didn't need to build barracks with the added plus that if the R.A.F. flew over, they wouldn't know which buildings housed Germans and which were inhabited by us innocent islanders.

However the R.A.F. did attack the airport buildings. Two houses, one to the north and the other the south, were hit by stray bombs. Luckily both families survived but it was decided that we lived too close to the airport and had to find safe shelter elsewhere at night.

My mother suggested that we go to the house in which she was born. It was empty as her brother and family had evacuated.

It was there that we found my uncle's abandoned cat and young kitten. Many animals were left behind to fend for themselves. The kitten stayed with us but was very frail, its mother survived by hunting for mice and had very little milk to give. To my immense upset the kitten didn't survive and the mother never returned after that.

My Most Terrifying Moment...

Food stocks were initially high due to so much of the island's population being evacuated... but food ran down quickly. Ration books were issued. It was I who had to collect the rations for us. We were registered with Mrs de Beaucamps who now lived three miles away as her house was uninhabitable from the R.A.F. bomb.

The German soldiers were amazed by what was available in the shops. They bought many things to ship home - so much so the Postal Service couldn't cope. All of the food and clothing leaving the island meant there was little left for us.

There were queues in the shops. If a soldier entered he would jump the queue and demand to be served first. If the shopkeeper refused, he would be reprimanded and if repeated, the shop would be closed and he might be sent to a camp in France or Germany.

Another item that was soon in short supply was clothing. Shops had little left and the German shopper was the main cause of this so shirts for men were hard to find. People who had clothes they didn't really need swapped them for other items.

Stepfather's brother who lived a few miles away needed a shirt; he was desperate. Luckily we had one to spare and I was given the important task of delivering it under strict instructions to be as fast as I could as the article was of great value.

I got my bicycle out and holding the precious brown paper bag firmly on the handlebars, I began my important mission.

Cycling past the airport, I headed down the Chêne Hill onto the main Forest Road. We had been informed by the German masters that all vehicles now had to be driven on the right-hand side of the road. This also applied to bicycles.

After about two miles I had to leave the main road and turn sharp left to enter a narrow winding lane bordered by high hedges that descended to a granite farmhouse with a low wall out front before sweeping away in the opposite direction.

As I sped downhill I wondered - why should I obey foreign orders? I would ride on the left-hand side as normal. I really felt brave with no care in the world.

Unfortunately, unknown to me and hidden by the high hedges, descending rapidly from the other side was a German soldier on his bicycle. It wasn't until we reached the bend in front of the farmhouse that we saw each other and it was too late to take evasive action.

We collided and both ended up on the road. The soldier uttered words I did not understand but the movement of his right hand towards his pistol I understood with frightening clarity.

Even though I was in some pain, I managed to get up and run quickly up the way I came, diving into the first gateway I found. I risked a glance to see if the soldier had followed me but to my immense relief he was still brushing down his tunic.

He then hurled my bicycle against the wall and released the air from the tyres before doing something that made my heart stop; he picked up the brown paper bag I had dropped. I prayed that he wouldn't take it, leaving my mission with no chance of completion.

Fortunately he didn't look inside and flung the bag over the nearest hedge before picking up his own bicycle, adjusting the handlebars and riding on his way up the hill past me.

As soon as I felt it was safe to do so, I headed out and back down to my bicycle with two flat tyres. Enquiring at the farm house I asked to retrieve the parcel from the garden where it was flung. The lady asked no questions, which was odd but I then realised in the one room house she had probably heard the whole commotion.

Happily, the bag was easy to find; it's resting place atop a large cabbage! I was then able to push my bicycle the two hundred yards to deliver the package to the man for which it was intended. I was then able to borrow a pump and head home, this time on the right side of the road.

I was frightened many times during the Occupation but I was never as scared as I was during that encounter with the enemy. My mother never did find out the trouble I'd had carrying out what had seemed a simple task and luckily, I was never asked to deliver anything of such importance again.

The German Presence.

The German soldiers continued to train and went on many route marches. Their objective was still the invasion of England and they were confident they would achieve it.

We later learned that before they arrived on the island they were put under instruction to be on their best behaviour so that we could then tell the people in the UK how the Germans weren't all bad - that they may not pay cricket but you'll get on well enough when they arrive. Thankfully this never happened - they decided to go east instead.

German Luftwaffe troops marching along Glategny Esplanade, St Peter Port, 1940
© *Guernsey Museums & Galleries*

School

The days of summer in 1940 were warm and our holiday was long. We even wondered if we would ever go back to school.

The States of Guernsey would have known how many children of school age had been evacuated but were unsure how many students or teachers had remained. They also needed to know how many schools were available because many were being used as barracks for their soldiers.

Eventually the States found about 1000 children of school age and coaxed teachers out of retirement to fill the vacant schools. My nearest school was down the road in St Pierre-du-Bois and I was delighted that our teacher was Mrs Lainé, who was known to us.

Mrs Lainé and my class.

It was late autumn and the weather was cold. The small fire we had at the school was totally inadequate. We had to provide a bottle which was filled with milk and placed near the fire to keep warm.

For the bread we were told that bakers were running out of flour and that potatoes would be used as a supplement. Mr Lainé assured us that we wouldn't find a whole potato in the centre of the loaf! It would be mashed and mixed with a smaller amount of flour.

As tooth powder was scarce, she also suggested that soot was to be used instead. This advice we received with groans of dismay.

All was going well, we were enjoying ourselves playing games and even had a football team.

I was nicely settled in and getting used to having girls in the classroom, when we were told we had to leave the school as it was required for more soldiers arriving in the island.

Our school body was split roughly in two; one group to the school in the parish of St Saviour to the north and the other to Torteval in the south.

I was sent to St Saviour's School and I wasn't happy when I found that I'd been placed in a class with children much younger than me and not up to the standard of those I'd left.

On the first day the teacher handed us a new exercise book and gave us a dictation. I was determined to prove to the head teacher than I should be in a higher class and wrote in my best joined-up handwriting, without a single smudge or blob of ink on the page.

The next day the exercise book was returned and to my shock the page was roughly torn out. The head teacher came up to me and I was told that I should have printed my words like the others.

I told her that I had not been informed of this and hadn't done printed writing for ages, for which she took an instant dislike to me and demanded I go back to printing.

Every day she would come up to me and see how I was getting on with what I regarded as a backwards step. She would peer over my shoulder and shout corrections to my lettering, accompanied by a heavy slap across my ears.

I was no longer enjoying school but relief from this unbearable ordeal was soon at hand from a very unlikely source. The cavalry? The German Army. They needed the school and so I was sent on to Torteval School and thankfully the head teacher went elsewhere. That is one thing I shall always be grateful to them for.

The school in Torteval had us packed in like sardines. It was very boring; daily copying out of a book. This upset Mother who had already spent a lot of money on my education, only for it to be wasted.

Other parents, too, were not satisfied with the way their sons were being educated and approached Brother Victor, Director of Les Vauxbelets College, and asked if he would consider reopening the school. He was the only teaching brother left as all the others were off-island but he agreed nonetheless.

Mother got a place for me there in January 1942. We walked over two and half miles on icy roads to reach what was the largest school on the island.

I joined eleven other boys there and soon returned to all the subjects we loved; French irregular verbs, algebra, Shakespeare and others.

Fortunately in the valley below the brothers ran an Agricultural College and the farm buildings were far superior to any of the others on the island. Before the war many boys from Europe were educated there.

Many more boys soon joined and in the large room we were divided into three groups according to age. I was in the top group and Brother Victor would begin with us and talked for half an hour, then move on to the others. He was a brilliant teacher and we all behaved as we were all eager to learn.

In the grounds of Les Vauxbelets is the smallest chapel in the world, built in the 1930s by Brother Deodet. The walls are covered with pieces of crockery and ormer shells. There is a long meadow opposite, with a steep bank on the other side, which was our playing field that we shared with cows and at one end, cider apple trees.

We would often take large metal hoops we'd found on the farm to the top of the bank and race them down the bumpy slope.

In the autumn the cider apples were picked and the cider press in one of the barns was put to use. The apples were crushed and the lovely juice flowed into a wooden barrel.

During the lunch hour whilst the Brothers were eating, some of us would sneak into the barn and help ourselves to the delicious cider.

However it didn't take Brother Victor long to notice that some of us were far less attentive than they had been in the morning! He soon realised the cause after some boys went as far as to fall asleep.

He took immediate action and one of the farm Brothers was posted on duty to protect the lovely cider. Our small avenue of pleasure was swiftly cut off.

Looking back, it was just as well that Brother Victor did this, otherwise we might have all ended up incurable alcoholics.

One day a German Officer called whilst we were in the classroom. He was a member of their military police. He explained that the reason for his visit was that two boys wearing our school caps – blue with two red hoops – were seen leaving a German store with stolen food.

This was a very serious offence and liable to severe punishment. He wanted the two culprits to stand up but no one moved.

One boy suggested that the two thieves were wearing the college caps to throw suspicion on members of the school. The officer nodded agreeing that it might be the case, but thinking it unlikely.

He and Brother Victor left the room and through the windows we could see them walking in deep conversation. They were there for ages. We were worried that if the officer was convinced that it was two of us, how we might be punished.

After what seemed like an awfully long time, Brother Victor came back to the room alone. He told us not to worry as he had persuaded the officer that no boys from his school would do such a thing. There was a huge sigh of relief all around. However, he warned that if the culprits were in the room that he would not be able to save them if they repeated the crime.

Food Supplies

Food was getting short and trips to the shops were often in vain. The Germans, on the other hand, were bringing in food from France. Although they still took local milk, cream and butter from us. We were lucky if we were able to get even skimmed milk. Farmers, however, were still allowed to keep some full cream milk for themselves.

Meat was in very short supply but many suppose that we must have had fish, being surrounded by the sea. I truthfully do not remember eating any during the Occupation.

Not long after our German visitors arrived, some fishermen tried to escape to England under the guise of going fishing. This infuriated our enemy and they ordered all fishing boats to be taken to St Peter Port harbour, no matter their condition.

They did eventually relent to allowing fishing but there were strict rules. Any fishermen wishing to go fishing alone could do so but only in good visibility and they couldn't stray more than one mile from the shore. They also had to be married with a wife on island; the idea being that no man would abandon his wife. Some fishermen who took soldiers on board could go as far as three miles but curfew still applied.

Sometimes a fair amount of fish could be caught but the soldiers took most of the catch. Occasionally enough would be caught that some could be sold at the fish market. If Mother got word of the fish, I was told to cycle into town to get some but as we lived five miles from the market, by the time I got there all the fish was inevitably gone. After a few unsuccessful attempted trips, we gave up trying.

Limpets were collected from the few rocks that were accessible without risk of mines but as there were so few, none of those ever reached us either. The closest I came to having produce from the sea was jelly made from carrageen moss collected from the rocky shores.

It contained no sugar or flavourings making the first spoonful very hard to swallow but it had to be eaten as there might not be anything else.

The German Authorities were soon reminded that they were obliged to bring in food for the civilians. This meant that eventually they allowed Mr Falla and one or two others to go to France and purchase food, medication, footwear and anything else they could find. Naturally, they had to be fluent in French and even then it wasn't easy as the French were also running short on food and clothing.

Seed for crops was given high priority, occasionally flour, sugar and even pork was bought. An incredible feat under the circumstances! Getting them shipped to Guernsey was even more difficult. Surprisingly, our health remained fairly good, even though there was a shortage of solid foods.

We ate a lot of vegetables, more than we ever did pre-war. This, however, brought a looseness of the bowels and for many this meant frequent trips to 'la petite maison' at the bottom of the garden. Not ideal in the middle of winter!

We all benefited from a healthier lifestyle. People lost weight as they had to cycle or walk everywhere. Heart and lung problems seemed to improve and visits to the doctor were few and far between. Despite this, people were not as physically strong and this made it harder to undertake strenuous jobs.

One of the most disparaging things was that sometimes there was a shortage of water, as supply was cut off. This made it difficult to keep the bathroom and kitchen in a clean and healthy state.

Chocolate and Cabbage Soup

Nowadays, when I give talks on the Occupation, the one thing that children can't seem to fathom is that I didn't have more than one pound of chocolate during the whole occupation.

How long can they go without? A week, is the invariable reply.

I tell them it helped me grow big and strong; I am no weakling.

I also ask them how they feel about cabbage soup.

This was a staple in our diet. Mother made it several times a week, with no meat or even salt added as there was none available. A few herbs would be sprinkled over the cabbage.

All our vegetables were grown organically and sometimes I was lucky enough to find a juicy slug among the leaves I was eating. This was my protein.

They are never impressed.

I always make the point of saying that anyone who can't do without chocolate and hates cabbage soup, in my opinion, would not have survived the Occupation.

Favours for Food

Halfway through the Occupation a family took possession of an empty cottage near us. There were two boys my age and we became friends. They had two sisters older than us.

I was invited over quite often and one thing that drew my attention was that they always had more food than us and some of it was not on rations. I loved going there as sometimes when their parents were out I was invited in and given food by the boys that was unavailable at our house. They didn't always have this special food but when they did the boys were exceedingly generous.

On one occasion I mentioned this extra food to Mother and she only said she was not surprised. I could tell by the sound of her voice that she didn't approve either. However, she did not elaborate. Not long after, quite by chance, I discovered the reason for their supplementary sustenance.

I was on one of my favourite walks by the airport where a long track led to many fields and to two streams that converge. It was very peaceful and quiet with no roads or houses.

It was a beautiful sunny day and skylarks sang. I had only gone about two hundred yards when I could hear unusual noise from a field. Peering over the hedge, what I saw shocked me even though I knew precisely what was happening.

At the far end of the field one of the older sisters of my friends was lying with a German soldier. I called out to her and she bolted upright and ran towards the far entrance to the field, trying to right her clothes.

Now I knew exactly what my mother meant when she said she wasn't surprised that they had extra food.

I later worried that she had recognised my voice but on one of my regular visits to their cottage both she and the soldier were there and neither showed any inkling that they knew it was me. Just as well as it meant I could still enjoy the extra food!

Claude Ozanne

Although German soldiers occupied many of the empty houses, some that were still occupied by locals were requisitioned too – usually those of a higher quality.

One day as we were having tea, we heard a loud knocking on the outside door, opening it to a booming voice with a strong accent declaring that they wanted our house and we had two days to remove our furniture.

Not only had they taken our car but now our house… and what next?!

Fortunately the new occupants were officers who wanted a new house with electric lights, a telephone and a bathroom that had hot water so if we ever got our house back it might even be in an improved state!

The immediate problem was to find somewhere to store our furniture. Luckily, Stepfather knew a farmer who lived nearby. He had a barn that was empty and it was offered to us.

No house and no furniture. We still needed somewhere to live. Stepfather had a nephew, Claude Ozanne, who lived at the lower end of our lane and he invited us to stay with him. He had plenty room as his wife and two sons had been evacuated. Two sons! If only they had still been there!

Claude was pleased to have us not only as company but also as Mother could keep the house clean, look after the vegetable garden and cook the meals.

One evening, Claude and I went to visit a farmer friend of his who lived nearby. He lived alone as his wife and child were also away. There was a roaring fire to keep us warm and we all had a cup of hot milk – full of cream! Something I hadn't had for ages. They both had something from a bottle added to theirs to 'stave off the cold' or so I was told. It seemed they needed quite a lot!

When we left it was dark and well past curfew time. A hundred yards further down the road at Le Manoir, many soldiers lived in wooden barracks. In front of the large manor house there were a few tall pine trees and a tall wooden tower was built in an attempt to survey the South Coast. This area was heavily guarded, especially at night.

Fortunately as we walked towards the sentries, it was pitch dark. Nevertheless it was important that we were absolutely silent so that we weren't shot. Claude had soft-soled shoes whereas I had shoes sent by Mr Falla from France; they had thick wooden soles with cheap leather above.

Claude had had one strong drink too many and none to gently demanded I take off my 'blasted shoes' and I took his advice, even though walking on the tarmac was painful. It was only once we were well past and turned into Rue Perrot that I could put them back on. Suffice to say that Mother was not pleased at our lateness when we returned.

The Goat

We stayed with Claude for many months and got on extremely well. I found a few new friends and visited their houses but still spent a lot of time on my own.

It was then that Claude decided to buy a goat. She was young and frisky and I was given the task of looking after her. She was tethered most of the day but sometimes I let her loose. She followed me everywhere. What she liked most was playing a game of hide and seek. I would tell her to count to one hundred and then come and find me. The house was surrounded by trees and many shrubs. There were glasshouses, sheds and many other places for me to hide but no matter where I hid, she would find me quickly. I assumed that this was because she had a gift for sniffing people out.

One day I was heading out with no time to play our game but swiftly gave in to her sad eyes, promising just a quick one.

I took her to the usual starting point and hurried round the corner, about to hide behind a large rhododendron when I looked back towards the house and saw her peering at me. She quickly retreated when she saw me looking.

I marched straight up to her, pointing accusingly as I declared her a cheat. Now I knew how she had always found me so quickly! I took her back to the field and banged in the metal stake for her tether with a wooden mallet.

At the end of this patch of grass there was a short row of cabbages that had gone to seed. This was vital because if we wanted cabbages next year, some had to be left to produce seeds. Claude had warned me that whenever I moved the goat I had to make absolutely sure that she couldn't reach them.

Steve, a new friend of mine, showed up at the house without warning and asked if I'd come with him to his father's farm so he could show me a small thrashing machine he had made from wood.

I changed my clothes and headed to the farm with him, some two miles away, as we cycled he mentioned to me he'd moved the goat as she had nothing to eat, for which I thanked him and thought no more about it.

When I returned home, Claude was waiting for me. He fiercely led me to his precious cabbages – or where they once were; there were none to be seen.

He was angry but I knew that blaming Steve would not help. Thankfully, all was not lost as Claude's friend Jack had some cabbage seed to spare and gifted us with a generous handful.

I learned a valuable lesson there; never trust anyone completely. Even though Steve was a farmer's son, I should still have gone back to make sure that the goat had been moved correctly.

The goat that caused all the trouble!

A Multi-Cultural Experience with Black Market Trade

The Germans brought over thousands of slave workers to build the fortifications. Many were Poles, Russians and Spaniards who had fought on the losing side during the Spanish Civil War.

In the field next to Les Vauxbelets College many wooden huts were built to house the slave workers who were tunnelling into the hillside below. The German Underground Tunnels, or Underground Hospital as they are now known, were the longest tunnels in the islands. Many workers died as they were physically totally unsuited to the work.

Others were brought in voluntarily. They were trades people like electricians, plumbers and carpenters. Most of these were French, paid well and could afford to pay for accommodation with local families. They were even allowed to go home for short breaks.

Claude met two of these men and as they were looking for somewhere to stay and offered them his spare room.

One was from Paris and the other from Bayonne in the Basque region of South-West France. We soon learned the perks of this when the man from Paris took a short break back to France and returned with many different items. Among these were boxes of camembert cheese, packets of Gaulaise cigarettes and bottles of potent liqueurs like crème de menthe and Cointreau.

Most of what he brought he would sell on to black-marketers who would in turn sell them to civilians at very inflated prices. He did however bring out some camembert, liqueur and cigarettes to share with us after supper and the room soon filled with smoke.

We tucked into the cheese whilst the adults washed it down with the liqueurs and there was a really friendly atmosphere. The conversation was conducted solely in French with not a single English word to be heard. The Basque gentlemen soon offered me a drop of Cointreau, which I accepted but rapidly wished I hadn't. The room began to rotate and I felt drowsy. All I can remember after that point is Mother dragging me to bed. I took quite a while to recover.

Bread would have gone nicely with the cheese but it was scarce. Claude and Stepfather were allowed one pound loaf a week because they did manual work. Mother had none even though she worked in the vegetable garden, did the housework and washed all the clothes by hand with an evil smelling soap Mr Falla had sent from France. This was not regarded as work and neither was my school work or helping out.

At meal times, the men would cut themselves a slice of bread and eat as I looked on. Each day they would cut a 'U' shape into their bread before they left for work so that no one could take any.

My mother, however, was clever and after they departed she would fetch one of the loaves, cut a slice for me and then carefully imitate the mark that was there before. She was quite impartial, rotating the loaves. I never knew if the men found out, if they did it was never mentioned.

The black markets flourished in Guernsey, as they did in many occupied territories. Ships travelling to and from ports in France brought in large amounts, usually by the French like the ones staying with Claude and also German soldiers who wanted to supplement their income.

Unfortunately, these sought after items went to those who could afford the high prices and those that had lost weight began to put it back on!

From 1942 the black market spread and farmers had more to eat than us. One farmer I knew admitted to me that all his eggs were sold to German soldiers, as they got more for them.

Potatoes were always in short supply, although not all were eaten. The ends of the potato, where the 'eyes' are, were saved and planted.

Some animals were slaughtered illegally and the meat sold for expensive prices. Tea and sugar were also luxuries whilst a single pound of flour could fetch £20.

One day, a man we know came to us with a bottle of red wine. There was nothing on the bottle to indicate where it came from and he wanted £4 for it. When the bottle was shaken there was so much sediment that you could not even see the colour of the wine. We refused to purchase but he kept on and on, desperate to get rid of it.

It seems he was a known alcoholic who knew the wine was undrinkable and wanted the money to buy one that was. The back and forth went on long enough that when he left, he had surely aged a few years.

Tobacco

Stepfather managed to get seeds of tobacco plants. He had a greenhouse two hundred feet long and thirty feet wide that was soon filled with them.

The leaves were cut and dried, then sliced and saltpetre added so that it would burn. I would go round greenhouses where men were working and sell a packet for one Reichmark.

I did rather well at this new venture, although Mother never found out what I was doing.

Cures for Boredom?

There were long periods of inactivity in the war and while this did lower morale among the soldiers, Guernsey was still an ideal posting for them.

Official brothels were opened in St Peter Port with girls brought in from France to cure the boredom of the soldiers and queues of them outside these houses was a source of amusement for locals.

One man opened a bar in a house that had been vacated by evacuees. He did a roaring trade. He also sold bottles of water that had been sweetened. I bought a bottle once, there was no flavour and it tasted foul. I never went there again.

Past-Times

Although I had friends, I still enjoyed spending time on my own. On week days I spent very little time at home, particularly during the summer holidays, I would return for meals and then be off out again.

I would wonder the fields and sometimes cycle to St Peter Port.

One cinema was open – 'The Gaumont' in St Julian's Avenue. Only a few films in English remained in the island. There was a cowboy film I liked and another entitled 'Saturday's Heroes' about an American football team.

Films in German were advertised outside the building and one day I decided to see what they were like. Within the cinema we were segregated in the stalls by a long pipe that ran all the way down them. German soldiers on the left, civilians on the right. Looking over at the soldiers I could see that most were asleep. There were no subtitles so I had no idea what was being said; I didn't stay long. I never bothered to see another German film.

The Gaumont Palace cinema during the Occupation, the film 'Sieg im Western' was released in 1941 about the campaign against France.
© *Carol Toms / Guernsey Museums & Galleries*

Luckily a Guernsey company put on shows at the Lyric Theatre in New Street. They were musicals with humorous content. One of the songs that still lingers with me went 'I lift up my finger and say tweet-tweet chou-chou now-now come-come...' I haven't ever heard it since. I could only go to the matinees because of curfew.

There were also military band concerts in Candie Gardens that were of no interest to me and sometimes there were football matches at the close by Cambridge Park between German and local teams.

I often went to Candie to enjoy the gardens which led down to a lower gate and a lane that twists its way to the so-called Blue Mountains. This was a lane that had been designated a no-go area but I couldn't contain my curiosity forever and decided to investigate the forbidden area.

After the first bend, the lane was uphill and straight. It was just as I rounded this corner that I immediately wished I had never thought to explore at all. Descending towards me were two German officers in deep conversation.

This might have been the only thing that saved me, giving me chance to flee back the way I had come and return to the lower gardens of Candie and flinging myself into the bushes to hide.

My heart was beating at an unhealthily fast rate as I waited for the inevitable sound of jackboots. I waited for at least half an hour before I decided that it was safe to leave. I shall never know if those officers saw me or not.

Choir

Buildings at the airport that were destroyed by the bombing were very close to two churches. In 1942 the Parish Church reopened and I was invited to join the choir as the rector wanted more male voices.

I wore a cassock, white surplice and a stiff white collar with a black bow. I had to attend Sung Eucharist in the morning and Evensong. The services were well attended as we had an influx of Methodists from the church that remained closed.

Choir practice was on Friday evenings and to save electricity it took place in the vestry. Mr Wilson, the organist, had to cycle from town; four and a half miles. He told Mother that there was a shortage of vegetables there. Mother happily agreed to give him some and I found myself walking in the dark to choir practice with a small sack full of root vegetables.

At the cemetery in front of the church I saw someone standing in the darkness. I couldn't see them very well but enough to tell it was a German Officer. He could see I was carrying something and as I ran to the back of the church towards the vestry, he followed.

Rounding the last corner I threw the sack behind a tombstone as I entered the vestry. The door was flung open behind me as fast as I'd shut it as the officer barged in and surveyed the motley crowd of choristers. He seemed to find nothing untoward as he left just as quickly, without a word.

I told Mr Wilson that the sack of vegetables was behind a tombstone which got me an odd expression in reply but no outward comment. I left practice early, swinging my arms as I passed the still lingering soldier, to show I had nothing in my hands.

I was worried that our choirmaster might be stopped and searched but on Sunday's Evensong he thanked Mother for the vegetables with no mention of any problems with the officer.

Occasionally two German soldiers attended our evening services. This wasn't considered that odd as it was assumed that some members of the Third Reich had to be Christians.

They might have been but we later learned that the main reason for their presence was to listen to the Rector's sermon and ensure it was devoid of any anti-German content.

Fortifying Guernsey

For the German army, capturing British Soil in the form of the Channel Islands was a large feather in Hitler's cap and a step towards dominating Europe.

Our island became one of the most heavily defended territories in Europe, forming part of the Atlantic Wall.

It is said that over 200, 000 cubic metres of concrete was poured into the island as miles of tunnels were dug and many huge bunkers were built. The walls of these could be very thick and along the vulnerable coastline, even thicker anti-tank walls were built.

Hitler said that the Third Reich would last 1000 years and the fortifications that were built in Guernsey will last 1000 and more.

Many large guns were brought in with the largest being the four that made up the Mirus Battery. They came from a Russian Battleship of the First World War and certain roads had to be widened to get them into position.

Heavy guns being transported through St Martins en route to the Mirus Battery
© *Guernsey Museums & Galleries*

Huge casemates were built below ground with 66 soldiers in each, air conditioning and guns with a 360 degree field of fire at a range of 50 kilometres. Our house shook when they were fired.

On top of all of this, 60,000 mines were laid in the island. The South Coast cliffs and beaches were mined and we couldn't go for a swim. The beaches were out of bounds. On the cliffs lines of barbed wire and large signs proclaiming 'ACHTUNG MINEN' warned people of the danger.

One day I was walking along the cart track that bordered the mined area that leads to La Corbiéres. As I approached a bend, I heard young voices and I couldn't believe what I was seeing as I rounded the bend.

Two young boys had gotten through the barbed wire and were playing amongst the gorse… right where the mines were laid.

I hurried along and urged them to get out as they were in danger from the mines. They took no notice and laughed even more. I didn't know what to do; should I go in and remove them forcibly?

I was about to do so when the boys reached a row of tall gorse bushes that barred their way. As they could go no farther, they crawled back through the wires and onto safe ground.

I tried to instil warnings into them to never do that again but they just laughed and ran off. It was only as I walked on, praising myself for a job well done, that it suddenly occurred to me that if a mine had gone off then I would have been blown to smithereens too.

This made up my mind that I had to go a step further. I knew who the young boys were and immediately went to the home of one of them and told the father what had happened. He thanked me and I assumed the boy would follow his father's advice more than my own.

Both boys survived the Occupation, despite their dangerous games.

Raymond

Although I had now met quite a few children of my age, I never got that close to them. They remained acquaintances more than friends.

It was walking through the fields behind the farms one day that I came across Raymond, a boy I had previously only known vaguely from my earlier school days, as well as a younger boy named David.

To find someone my age living so close to me, on a farm, was a revelation and this coupled with his enthusiasm at seeing me led to us becoming fast friends.

The reason that I hadn't seen him around before was that he had to do more than his fair share of work.

Living so close, I went round most days except Sundays. He couldn't leave until he finished his chores so I gave him a hand so that we could go for a walk through Forest Parish.

He being the son of a farmer, and I the son of a grower, nearly everyone in the parish knew us and we were allowed to go through their farms at will. We climbed most of the trees in the parish; the Dutch elms were easy but the pines far more difficult. We hunted for nests, particularly those of magpies that were high in tall trees and the hardest to reach.

There were many streams running to the South Coat and we found one in particular that ran through an area known as Le Bigard, with a granite trough where the water ran remarkably clean. We were splashing the water around when the door to an old cottage opened and an old woman ran at us, shouting in French and waving a broom. We learned later that we had in fact been playing in her sole supply of fresh water - safe to say we did not go back.

Many times when I called at Raymond's farm home, there were many jobs to be done. Every morning the twelve cows had to be taken to the fields quite far from the farm. Raymond and I took six each through the deserted roads with little issue. Later the cows were milked. Upon asking if I could help, I was given a crash course.

I had to sit on a three-legged stool and was given an easily milked cow that could withstand the poor effort of a novice without reacting violently.

June was the month for collecting hay from the fields and Raymond and I were co-opted into the team of hay-makers. We sat on the hard wood of the horse driven cart through the quiet lanes as skylarks sang. It sometimes took half an hour to get to the fields and the journey was regularly quiet and peaceful. It seemed unfair that not so very far away there was a war raging and people were dying.

For the remainder of the Occupation Raymond and I spent the majority of our time together, he even joined me at Les Vauxbelets College.

Music & Lime

Nowadays, many people can't go a day without listening to 'popular' music constantly being played in restaurants, shops or being transmitted directly into a person's ears.

We only had the radio. During the first few months of the Occupation we were allowed to keep our radios but when Guernsey-born 2nd Lieutenants Nicolle and Symes were caught spying, the radios were called in as punishment. After a while they were returned to us but soon after they were confiscated once again.

Many people hid theirs. One of our neighbours who kept one was found out and sent to prison. We found out that someone had told the Germans about it as they didn't need to search the house for it; instead knowing the exact location.

Unfortunately this sort of behaviour was common but the perpetrators never discovered.

Four men who had worked in newspapers decided to produce a newsletter from the BBC news they listened to, calling themselves G.U.N.S. - Guernsey Underground News Service - but they were brought to the attention of the German Authorities and the men sent to a camp in Germany.

When we were allowed a radio we only listened to the news. After the last news of the day the National Anthems of the countries opposing the Nazis were played. Nothing else.

The radio ran on batteries; a 'wet' battery and a 'dry' one. The first could be recharged but once the latter was dead, there was no power. No radio, no music.

We went nearly five years without popular music; it was something we just had to put up with...but we survived.

Church music was about all we had and only on Sundays; Sung Eucharist in the morning, psalms and hymns in the evening.

Choir practice was on Fridays and knowing the hymns and psalms already, I taught myself the harmonium and would practice the songs on the organ.

On the occasions when Mr Wilson was unable to reach us on his bicycle, I was asked to play the church organ. In doing so I had in a small way achieved one of the two things Mother hoped I'd do.

I learned to play Handel's Largo and would pull out all the stops and play as loud as I could in my bedroom. One day I realised it was selfish of me to keep it to myself so I opened all the windows so that the rest of the parish could enjoy it with me. I was told that many windows remained firmly shut during my performance.

The church had many windows with coloured glass. One of the windows had glass that was the colour of lime. Whilst the Rector was delivering his sermon, my eyes would inevitably stray to the lime-coloured glass. Before the war, a lime drink was one of my favourites to enjoy. It was agony to be reminded of it and I had to continually force myself to look away, otherwise I might have had a breakdown.

Returning Home?

In 1943, some of the troops stationed in Guernsey were needed elsewhere and these included those who had taken up residence in our home. We left Claude's and finally repossessed our property.

The barn-stored furniture was returned and part of the house was painted so we settled in. Life was almost back to normal.

However soon Hitler realised that the garrison left behind were not up to strength and that left them vulnerable to an invasion by Churchill. This resulted in a new large number of soldiers sent to replace those that had left.

These soldiers were not of the standard of those that first arrived in 1940 but second-rate officers or not, they still wanted billets that were comfortable with mod-cons.

The inevitable knock on the door came once more and we were once again informed that our bungalow was required.

Claude offered us a return to his home, which had also been repainted. We decided it would be unfair to accept his kind offer but time was short and we needed to find accommodation quickly.

A short distance up the road were five cottages in a row. The previous occupants had been Germans that had now left, so they were available.

We contacted the owner who said we could choose one to occupy. All five were in a terrible state. We chose the one at the end even though it had an unhealthy smell to it, no bathroom and a toilet that was in a narrow shed at the far end of the garden.

The most annoying thing was that we had to pay rent for this ramshackle building, whilst our uninvited guests lived in our house rent-free.

After trying to survive there for a while, we came to the decision that what we had was unsafe and uninhabitable. We inspected the other four cottages and found one that was marginally better to move into. We put up with it while we kept an eye out for something better.

For a change luck favoured us. A larger detached cottage in the lane opposite our house became available. It had been occupied by locals, not the enemy but it still had no bathroom, an outdoor toilet and the rent reflected a more desirable dwelling.

Being able to see our home and yet never be allowed in was a feeling that was hard to swallow.

The Action I Still Regret

Being without even some of the simplest foods as we were during the Occupation, can lead to crazy cravings.

I was cycling past a blackthorn hedge after leaving a friend's house near St Saviour's Church when I noticed a thrush sitting on her nest.

I hadn't had an egg in so long that I had forgotten what one tasted like. I was overcome with the uncontrollable urge to have one.

I would wait until the thrush left her nest and take a single egg. I waited a long time; she didn't seem to want to leave and kept looking at me... probably aware of what I was up to. I decided to vanish around the corner and hope that she was gone when I returned. On my third try, the nest was finally vacant.

I looked inside and found only one solitary egg; light blue with black spots at the wide end. I picked it up to find it was still warm. Carefully I wrapped it in my handkerchief and deposited it into my saddle bag, riding home carefully.

Reaching home, I gave the egg to mother and asked if she could boil it. She dutifully did so and tried to hand it back to me but I couldn't take it.

I pictured the thrush looking at me. It immediately dawned on me what I had done. I had stolen her egg. I felt awful. I told Mother that I didn't want it and with a confused expression she ate it herself.

I got on my bicycle and hurried to the location of the nest, hoping that the thrush would be there for me to apologise to. She wasn't there. I returned home feeling sick. For the next few days I kept returning but there were no eggs in the nest and it had been abandoned, because of me.

I have never forgiven myself for what I did. That small egg would not have made any difference to me, hungry though I was... but it had meant a lot to the thrush.

Even now, there is still a small section of that hedge left and whenever I drive past I swear I see the thrush looking out at me. I am still utterly ashamed.

German

In the autumn of 1943 whilst at Les Vauxbelets College we were instructed by the German Authorities that we had to learn to speak German.

We weren't too happy with this so made little effort. Mr le Moigne, a local man, was given the unenviable task of teaching us unwilling boys. I felt sorry for him as he was a very nice man.

After a while we began to take an interest and did learn some German. We were told that 'ja' meant 'yes' as well as some useful sentences. However one sentence that I learned has never been anything but completely useless; stuck in my brain even now, taking up valuable space that would be better used by something else.

'Der Plattenspieler ist auf dem Tisch.'

'The record player is on the table.'

I learned this sentence in 1943 and still no one has ever asked me

"Wo ist der Plattenspieler?" to enable me to use my reply.

Although, to be fair, I would probably rather reply:

"Der blasted Plattenspieler ist kaput!" instead.

After a few months Mr le Moigne gave up and I resumed the task of improving my English.

Sports Day

As our sports ground was being used as an ammunitions dump, we had to hold our sports day in the meadow by the Little Chapel. It was uneven with uncut grass and the heifers had been tethered there not long before.

Our 'Sports Field' little unchanged in modern day – even still complete with an example of the Guernsey cows with which we shared it - making our games slightly hazardous! The Little Chapel can be seen on the left.

We were divided into teams and thoroughly enjoyed ourselves despite the hard-going terrain. The winners of the event were given a prize donated by parents and Vauxbelets' Old Boys.

I won the slow bicycle race on a borrowed bike for which I received a coloured vase which I still own, now knowing it is in fact a Clarice Cliff.

Bullets

Even though the war was not going to plan, the soldiers that occupied our main buildings above the Little Chapel continued to train, albeit not with great enthusiasm.

They were issued with both live and blank bullets. Many weren't used and they dare not go back with them so they took to throwing them into the shrubs above the chapel.

We would then gather them. The blanks had a wooden head painted red which we could remove and empty the powder onto a flat surface where we would shape it into a snake. One end of the powdered line was lit and the flame worked its way to the other quickly.

The live bullets were much more difficult to deal with. On one instance we reached a large granite bolder in the gateway to a field narrow lane overlooking the airport as we cycled home, giving us an idea to get rid of the bullets.

We placed the bullets one by one on the large boulder, using another sizeable piece of granite to set them off. We did this by standing legs apart above the bullets and dropping the stone onto them.

A farmer working in a nearby field heard the noise and came to investigate. When he saw what we were doing he was horrified and advised us to cease immediately. He took the remaining bullets and told us not to repeat such a stupid act. Just as well it was him rather than a soldier who had spotted us, as we would have had to explain how we got hold of the ammunition!

Resistance

One question that I often get asked about the Occupation is whether there was a resistance movement in the Island?

During the Occupation there were roughly 19,000 civilians and up to 16,000 fully armed troops. Direct opposition of the occupying forces would have been futile.

There was a form of passive resistance, with many rules and regulations issued by the German command not always being followed by our government. There were a very small number who collaborated but they were condemned.

Some young women formed relationships with the soldiers and many illegitimate children were born as there were few young Guernsey men on the island as they were serving in the armed forces.

It should be pointed out that there was no molesting of women as troops had been ordered to be on their best behaviour. Discipline was very strict and soldiers who stepped out of line would be punished.

There was one instance where a Guernsey woman was assaulted in her bedroom in town and reported it to the German command. To their credit they investigated and found the damning evidence in her room where the German had left his revolver. He was traced and admitted his guilt for which he was dispatched to a prison in France.

The Germans were suspicious of whether all the information they received anonymously was genuine and always made thorough investigations before acting, in some cases in extremes for the slightest reasons.

However there was one occurrence in 1943 where a great passive demonstration of our loyalty to the Crown left the Germans in no doubt to which side we were supporting.

On the night of 23rd October 1943, H.M.S. Charybdis and Limbourne were torpedoed and sunk. They had taken part in a disastrous operation off the North Coast of Brittany in France.

This led to an event which took the Germans completely by surprise; on a cold November afternoon bodies from this tragedy were washed ashore on Guernsey's beaches.

The Germans decided to show us that they were decent people by burying the dead with full military honours. Whilst they tried to down-play the funeral, word soon got around and five thousand of us turned up in comparison to the few officers and the firing squad that they had present.

A few of us boys from Les Vauxbelets turned up in our school caps and the Inspector of Police, being an Old Boy himself, escorted us to the front so that we had a better view of this important ceremony.

This large turnout did not go down well with the enemy and so when more bodies arrived, they too were buried with military honours but no local person was allowed into the cemetery, stopped by a large military presence.

It is important to note at this point that even this horrific event did not shake our faith that one day we would be liberated.

To this day a service is held every October at Le Foulon Cemetery with a large naval party in attendance.

The Funeral Service for the crew of H.M.S. Charybdis at Le Foulon Cemetery, St Peter Port on 17th November 1943
© *Guernsey Museums & Galleries*

Close-Up of the crowd in the above photograph, amongst whom I stood.

Deportation

Many people were deported from Guernsey to camps in Germany and France, the majority simply because they had been born in England. None, however, were related to us and so we remained unaffected by it until it was reported that Masons were to be collected and sent away.

Stepfather was a Mason and Mother was terribly worried that he would be taken. He was twenty years older than her and she feared for his survival in those conditions.

Fortunately, this idea was scrapped and we heard no more about it. It was rumoured that an agreement was reached between the Masons and the German Authorities. No one seems to know how this was achieved.

However, my now-wife's uncle was deported because they found out that he fought against them in World War I. He was tortured and even though he returned to the island he never recovered from his ordeal.

Many others were deported, several for obscure reasons. Men, women and children; no one was spared and not all returned.

A Quiet War

A lot was going on elsewhere during the war but nothing much went on for us; it was pretty quiet.

The daylight hours were short apart from Sundays when I had two church services to attend. In the dark winter hours I read books or coloured pictures but with only one writing pencil and a single sky blue crayon, I had little scope to improvise. On a reasonably fine day I would often visit David, one of my friends from before the war. Even though he had two sisters for company, he was always happy to have another boy to spend time with.

They had a glasshouse with a bench and a lot of tools. We made ourselves toys out of wood, although truth be told he was much better at it than I was. If it was dry we played a game that we invented. All we needed was a tennis ball and a road. The road running past the house suited us well as it was long and straight.

We would begin by standing twenty yards apart. The one who won the toss kicked off and the idea was to kick the ball as far as you could along the road, past your opponent. This meant that you had gained distance and he had to kick from where the ball stopped. The one who pushed his opponent to the end of the road won.

Our game always had few interruptions; occasionally a wooden German cart pulled by two strong French horses would pass us at a snail's pace but other than that the roads were rarely used.

An example of a German military wagon, photographed by C.H. Toms at the Albion Hotel near the Town Church in St Peter Port
© Guernsey Museums & Galleries

Sometimes we would play marbles in the middle of the road, placing them in a circle. The winner of the toss would flick one into the circle and remove as many as possible. These would now be his. If he missed, the other player would try. As neither of us had good glass marbles, we used to pick the oak apples off the tree at the edge of the gate and use those for our games.

Very occasionally our game was interrupted by a German tank. We would hastily gather up our 'marbles' as if a tank rolled over them they would never be fit for purpose!

Christmas Dinner?

One day not long before Christmas 1943, I decided to visit my old friend Raymond. There was a lot of snow and my boots sank as I traipsed across the fields. I watched as a magpie came down to land on the far side of a nearby hedge.

As I watched, it occurred to me that this would be our fourth Christmas under occupation and our fourth without a bird for Christmas dinner. It struck me that a plump magpie would sit nicely next to vegetables on our plates.

I made a mental note of where I thought the bird had landed on the other side of the low hedge, about five feet from a small tree.

Luck was with me and I found a fairly large chunk of granite. I moved forward to where I thought the magpie was. Having worked out the position as best I could, I threw the granite over the hedge and hoped it would hit the bird.

I waited, nothing happened. I thought that maybe I had caught it! Just as I was about to climb over the hedge to collect my prize I heard the flapping of wings and could only watch as the magpie flew away.

I was bitterly disappointed but consoled myself with the 'fact' that had the granite landed where intended, the bird would have been as flat as a pancake. It would then be useless for dinner and it also looked old and in all probability would have been as tough as old boots.

Cut off from Food

In June 1944, we could hear the bombardment on the coast of Normandy from Guernsey. We didn't know what it was until those who had made Crystal radios found out what was happening.

Further information arrived that the allies had established a foothold there and that everything was going well; we would be liberated soon... or so we believed. It would in reality be another eleven months.

Even direr was the fact that once the allies reached the ports of Granville and St Malo, we were cut off completely from the rest of the world.

It became obvious to the Germans that the Channel Islands were to be bypassed. In fact Churchill's idea not to try and take them back turned out to be a master stroke. All the soldiers and powerful guns and tanks on island could not be used to delay the allies' movement towards Germany.

The Germans had managed to bring in some food before their access was cut off but they had none for us.

Many of the workers brought in by organisation Todt to build fortifications were no longer needed as they had no materials to use.

Many of those that survived were returned to France. On Alderney, the only concentration camp on British soil, some of the prisoners were also removed.

Towards the end of September, food was running out for everyone. Mr Falla and the others were stuck in France and nothing could be sent over as the R.A.F. had complete mastery of the air.

We learned that as the civil population was British, the Germans had informed the British government that it was their duty to feed us. Churchill was not happy with this as he felt the food would just go to the German troops and not to us. We learned after the war that under international law it was not the British that were obliged to feed us after all.

By the autumn, food was in very short supply. Soap and clothing soon ran low too. Many times I would wash my hands with mud.

We still had vegetables but definitely not meat or bread. The soldiers had all the milk and meat for themselves. More glasshouses were taken over to produce vegetables for the enemy; kohlrabi was a favourite. The States of Guernsey also began using extra glasshouses for the growing of vegetables for those without gardens, with the bonus of giving Guernseymen some gainful employment.

In the south-west, the produce was delivered to a large shed at the Aeroplane Vinery overlooking the airport. I met a man who allowed me to join him as he collected fruit and vegetables. Sometimes there were lovely grapes in paper bags and as we rolled along the narrow lanes we would pluck a grape or two from the bag and eat them.

Raymond and I would go walking through gardens, inspecting them for food. Sometimes we got lucky and found ripe strawberries amongst the tall weeds and slugs. Thankfully gooseberries, raspberries and currents were easier to get to as they were above the weeds.

The few peaches we found were delicious, as were the small crops of apples and pears we helped ourselves to. We didn't regard it as stealing; the owners were miles away and if we didn't eat them then the enemy would!

If the Germans had surrendered, then food and essential items might have been allowed in but alas it was not a word that seemed to be in their vocabulary.

Cut off from Clothing.

Due to the shortage of food other than vegetables, people were rapidly losing weight. Clothes no longer fit and had to be altered as best we could.

Children were no longer allowed to take part in organised games and whilst we were confident at Les Vauxbelets that we had the best football team on the Island, we weren't allowed to prove it.

My shoes were too small; my toes couldn't stretch out and how Mother found clothes to fit me I don't know.

Two woollen cardigans were un-knitted and re-knitted into three. Two skirts altered into three.

I was given a pair of football shorts by Brother Victor that had belonged to a border who was now in England.

They were made with smooth material that was comfy to wear. They regularly disappeared and reappeared on the washing line and it was a while before I realised Mother had been wearing them as underwear!

Women's lingerie was also made out of the parachutes that were attached to the leaflets dropped by the R.A.F. at night, updating us on the progress of the allies in France.

Because of curfew, these were difficult to harvest as German soldiers frequently gathered them up before locals could get to them but luckily they never found them all.

A Foreign Friendship Makes a Difference

There was one soldier, although not an officer, who wielded great power in the German ranks in Guernsey. I would say he was probably the equivalent of a Regimental Sergeant Major in the British Army.

He had his quarters in a house in Le Bigard, Forest and we often met in the lanes. He would always stop for a chat in good English. He once told me that the reason he liked talking to me was that I reminded him of his son who was my age and he hadn't seen for over three years. I had blue eyes and blonde hair; the very image of his son.

One day, as I passed the observation tower amongst the pine trees at Le Manoir, he appeared and led me to the base of the tall tower. He began to mount the ladder and invited me to follow.

I was frightened and hesitated. I knew that things were not going too well for the German Army in France and if I reached the top he could very well throw me down.

I made the decision to trust him and followed. At the summit, there were two soldiers who, upon sighting their superior, stood smartly to attention.

My 'friend' pointed out to sea and I could just about see vessels of the Royal Navy towards the bay of St Malo. You couldn't make out which they were; just small black objects at sea.

I knew what they were. I also knew that he knew that I knew who they were.

I looked at him and without comment he just smiled and pointed to the exit.

It is quite possible that I was the only civilian in Guernsey to witness the heart-warming scene, all thanks to that soldier.

What I didn't know at the time was that our 'friendship' would save me, Mother and Stepfather from possible imprisonment.

It wasn't long after that the officers occupying out bungalow unexpectedly left, allowing us to move back in. The house was immaculate. Each bedroom now had a washbasin connected to the hot water boiler. We had our bathroom back and, as an added bonus, no rent to pay!

Many other houses like ours that had been occupied by non-locals were now available once more to their true owners.

Why the soldiers suddenly vacated these premises is unknown. One possibility is that things were going badly in Northern France and they feared the worst if they occupied our homes to the bitter end; reprisals by the owners would be justifiable once the war was over.

Although we settled well back into familiar surroundings, there was still an uncomfortable feeling in the pit of our stomachs that our house might once more be repossessed.

It did not worry us unduly until one night when an unfortunately familiar foreign banging on the outside door echoed through the house.

As we answered the door and went out of the house it was clear we were in serious trouble.

The conservatory, with its glass roof and front, was lit up – not only illuminating our yard but also further afield.

I had gone in earlier to fetch something, switched on the light and forgotten to turn it off as I left.

The German leader of the group was quick to point out the seriousness of the situation. The possibility of passing the rest of the war locked up somewhere went rapidly through my mind.

Stepfather quickly switched off the light and a torch lit up my face. The sergeant looked as if he was going to arrest us on the spot for disobeying quite possibly one of the most important regulations.

Before he did anything rash, one of his party whispered in his ear. He stared hard at me for a while. He looked closely at my face in the dim light. He smiled at me then, recognising me as the 'friend' of that Regimental Sergeant Major. It seemed sending me to prison might not be a smart move for his career.

He then informed me that they could overlook it this time due to my age but that if anything was to happen again then I would be dealt with most severely.

Knowing the right people could be useful.

Making Friends with the Enemy.

The locals and soldiers all became more relaxed as we waited to the inevitable end of the conflict. We were all in the same boat, so to speak. Soldiers had little to do other than wander about the parishes.

One day, as we were walking down our lane on our way to visit Claude, we met an older soldier. His uniform was unbuttoned and unwashed. He put his hand in his pocket and pulled out a crumpled photograph. He proceeded to explain in broken English that this was his family, that he hadn't seen them in many years, that none of the soldiers wanted to be here.

They were the words of a man who knew that the battle was lost. A complete opposite to the attitudes in 1940 when they saw themselves as the victorious army about to take over the world.

It was another such soldier that asked me my name once and when I proudly told him that it was 'Frederick' he declared that is was 'like Frederick ze Great, King of Prussia' and from then on I was given this nickname by those billeted in our area.

A young officer that lived opposite us with the homeowners, in what had been a guest house, became friendly with us too.

The owners must have told him that I collected stamps because he came round and offered to give me some that he had. I showed him my modest collection – as no more letters had arrived after the cut-off from Europe my collection had been cut short – and he told me that when he was my age he too had collected stamps.

Waiting for the end...

In the autumn of 1944, very little was happening in the Channel Islands. It was a very strange feeling. Nothing of the death and destruction in Northern France was felt here; only boredom and loneliness.

Sometimes Raymond and I would enter unoccupied houses, some of which had been used by soldiers. Furniture was missing and floorboards had been ripped up and used for firewood. Some houses were nearly empty.

It was not only soldiers that had removed items; relatives and friends who had stayed on the island helped themselves to things they wanted or needed.

After the war, returning evacuees were shocked at the state of their properties and even more so on finding precious possessions in the homes of others. Some things were returned and some were not; some forgave and some never spoke to each other again.

To be fair, we had now reached a point where almost everything was wearing out and we had nothing in the shops with which to repair them.

Bicycles were the fastest mode of transport we had but once they needed repairing it was back to walking if nothing was available.

The inner tubes of my bicycle were rotten and couldn't be repaired. Fortunately, as growers we had long rubber hoses to water plants in the glasshouses. I had seen a few bicycles using hoses as substitutes for tyres.

I measured the periphery of the wheel and cut the exact length of hose to fit it. Then with a bradawl I pierced holes where the ends met and threaded wire through, twisting the end as tight as I was able so that the hose wouldn't leave the wheel. It worked as a tyre but it was hard going, especially uphill as I had no gears to help.

Returning home from school was hardest as the hills were steep. I was too weak to make it more than halfway up and had to dismount and push the bicycle to the top.

As the weather got colder and the daylight shorter, we needed wood for the cooker that provided us with hot water. I knew of a valley about two miles away, mostly populated with blackthorn trees.

Mother, Stepfather and I borrowed a large handcart and with the help of a saw we eventually had enough wood to fill it. Pushing the heavy cart uphill needed a massive effort when under normal conditions we would have done this easily.

A few weeks later we returned to that valley for more wood. This time pushing the cart was even harder as a lot of rain had fallen and the track from the valley was muddy. Because we were even weaker, we couldn't push the cart back up the steep hill to get us to road.

It looked as though we would have to abandon our load. We waited a while to catch our breath. We made one more attempt but had no luck.

As we moved off without our precious load, a man appeared offering help. We explained that there was no way that we could get our cart home. With his help we managed, little by little, to get the wheels moving up to a drier part of the track and then onto the hard surface of the lane.

We thanked him for his help but when he found out we had another mile to go, he refused to take no for an answer and declared he would help us the rest of the way.

We gave him a sandbag full of vegetables and our profound thanks for all his help. It is certain we would not have made it home without him.

He never introduced himself and I still don't know who he was but without his help our cart would have been left to rot at the bottom of that valley.

Nearing the end...?

In the autumn of 1944, not only food but other things were in short supply; such as soap and clothing. We still had vegetables but no milk or bread and the Germans had all the meat and dairy.

It had been this way for so long that we had no idea how long this would continue and whether it would end with us starving.

We were, of course, completely unaware of what was going on behind the scenes between the British and German governments over who would supply us with food. It wasn't until after the war that this was revealed.

With the Germans' plans to use us as a stepping stone across Europe halted, we became even more isolated due to the loss of many of the German ships that supplied the Island.

After D-Day, we hoped that we would be liberated within two or three months. This didn't happen. Once the allies had stormed down the Contentin Peninsula to Granville and St Malo, all the ports used by the Germans were completely cut off. What followed was the worst eleven months of the occupation.

The German garrison was going to be starved out. The presence of the Royal Navy in the area suggested this. The only way we could survive was off the land; nothing else was going to be available to us for quite a while.

We heard that the Germans thought that if the local population could be removed, there would be more food for them. This decision was taken too late and so nothing happened.

Had the German garrison surrendered, it would have made life easier for us but they were not going to give up our fortified island without a fight. There were about 13,000 troops here after D-Day who were prepared to fight to the last man.

Reclaiming Our School

In the winter of 1944, Les Vauxbelets College became vacant once more. We could finally leave the farm building and reclaim the school itself. As it had been occupied for four years by the lower ranks, it was left in a terrible state.

A room was found on the third floor that was in useable condition but a lot of stairs had to be climbed which was difficult for undernourished boys. Needless to say it wasn't long before a ground floor room was cleaned up to use.

The Red Cross

Our weakened states did not go completely unnoticed. There was a lot of haggling between the British and the Germans about who was going to get in touch with the International Red Cross in Geneva.

Eventually, we were allowed to do so. Thankfully the Red Cross lost no time in getting things organised. A Swedish ship, the SS Vega, was found to deliver us much needed aid.

Unfortunately, it wasn't until after Christmas that it arrived into our harbour in St Peter Port. There were something like 100,000 parcels from Canada and New Zealand and other items we urgently needed on board.

The Germans were asked to remove the parcels from the ship and distribute them around the island. They were trusted above the black-marketers, for had they got their hands on them, there would have definitely been less for us.

The discipline of the German army was such that they handed out the parcels far more fairly than expected.

Some of the most exciting items to arrive were soap that did not smell foul and require hours of running outside to relieve the smell and the bags of flour. Whilst I didn't like my clothes smelling bad and I had even used mud to wash my hands, I was more excited about the latter; I had forgotten what bread tasted like!

I was at school when the food provisions arrived at home. The boys living in St Peter Port had already received theirs. I had a carrot for lunch and whilst nutritious it did not compare to what the other boys had; sandwiches! I was deeply envious and couldn't wait to get home.

Normally, as it was uphill most of the way home, I would have to get off my bicycle and push it due to lack of energy and the hoses on the wheels.

With a massive effort that day, I managed to cycle all the way home. How I survived I shall never know!

On reaching home, I threw my bicycle down and rushed into the house to find my mother in the kitchen.

"Would you like bread and jam?" she asked me and I could hardly wait a second longer, breathless with excitement.

As I hadn't had bread for months and jam for years, this was like trying them new all over again. Those mouthfuls of bread and jam have never been bettered in all the years since.

We had a parcel each. I opened mine, from New Zealand.

There was a tin of SPAM and one of corned beef. Packets of dried eggs and dried milk. Thick round biscuits that needed to be soaked for hours before eating. Apricot jam! Still my favourite to this day. There was also a tin of condensed milk, coffee flavoured and sweetened. The idea behind it was to take a teaspoon and put it into a cup with hot water. I never did this; I simply took a spoonful and transferred it direct to my mouth. It was my parcel and I could do as I liked, however I always thought it a childish thing to have done.

Many, many years later at Castle Cornet, I met a man from Jersey who to my surprise admitted that he had eaten that coffee-flavoured condensed milk straight from the tin too! Perhaps it was not such a silly idea after all.

We all received one parcel a month after the initial one, without them I am sure that so many of us, including the Jerseyman and I, wouldn't have survived the sheer starvation.

Rabbits, Cats & Dogs

In early 1945, while we received food parcels, our captors and the men brought in for specialist jobs did not fare as well. There was an absence of meat on their tables and very few cows were slaughtered as they were needed for their milk.

There were plenty of rabbits on the five mile stretch of cliffs to the South but unfortunately no one could hunt them due to the thousands of mines the Germans had planted there. Not very good forward planning on their part.

It soon became apparent that pet cats and dogs owned by Islanders were disappearing. Although there may not have been as many as before, there was still a fair number and to lose pets in this way was extremely upsetting.

A friend once noticed a trail of blood that lead from their gate to a German gun emplacement and we soon realised what was happening to our beloved pets.

It is thought that at the end of the Occupation there were no cats left on the island. There certainly weren't many. We now had a cat and once we realised what was going on, Mother kept ours indoors at all times. The food parcels helped us keep it alive.

Another friend who was evacuated said on her return that the first thing she did was visit her grandmother who she hadn't seen for five years. She remembers her having a big fluffy black cat that had survived.

It didn't take long for the cat population to return to normal.

Other Uses for Food Parcels

One day, not long after we started receiving the food parcels, we were by our front gate when a cyclist approached and stopped to greet us. He was French and happy to chat in his language. He lamented his boredom and the awful food he had to endure.

As we spoke, I examined his bicycle. It was in surprisingly good condition and unlike mine, he had actual inflatable tyres! Mother also noticed and enquired about a sale.

His reply was that he wasn't interested in a sale but he would let me have it in exchange for a few good meals.

My mother accepted this offer and invited him in, frying onions and bully beef in a pan and cooking potatoes and carrots in a saucepan. He was also given a slice of bread and a cup of coffee. The expression on his face reflected his pleasure.

I don't remember how many meals he had but I do remember how it felt to ride a bicycle with real tyres. It took me a while to get used to it as there were no brakes.

When I first tried it out in our yard, I found I couldn't stop. The Frenchman just laughed and caught the bicycle before I fell off. He explained that in order to stop I had to turn the pedals backwards.

The Game I'm Not Allowed to Forget

Our quality of life improved tremendously with the food parcels; we no longer had to substitute dried parsnips for coffee or crushed bramble leaves for tea. Limpets were no longer prised off the rocks and jelly made from carrageen moss abandoned.

Even though we were regaining some strength, we were still denied taking part in organised games at school.

However it didn't stop us from arranging a game of football against a rival gang. We managed to find a pitch and a referee. I had no football boots, so I had to borrow Mother's ankle-length rubber boots even though they were far too big. Even laced up, I couldn't make them a tight fit.

If we were defeated, our reputation would be damaged beyond repair. It was not a game but a battle. Yet with only minutes to go, there was still no score.

I was the main attacker and I found myself with the ball in a favourable position just before the end. I dribbled through the opposition's defences until there was only the goalkeeper between me and glory.

I took aim and hit the ball as hard as I could, however it was not the ball that crossed into the goal - that flew over the crossbar. What did end up in the back of the net was my wellington boot! I have never been allowed to forget that awful blunder.

Hope for Liberation

As we approached spring 1945, across the Channel, our allies were moving at a steady pace and the Germans were retreating on all sides. There was optimism in the air that we would soon find release from our prison environment.

However, in the backs of our minds there were doubts. There were things we needed to know; would our liberation be quick and painless? How quickly would the enemy be removed from our island? How would the Germans react if the British demanded unconditional surrender?

We hoped the island would not be taken back by force, as there were bound to be many casualties amongst us islanders, particularly as there were nearly as many soldiers as civilians.

It has been suggested by some that our lack of active resistance to the Germans was a disloyalty to Britain, however it is to be noted that in keeping thousands of German troops with guns and tanks away from the ranks protecting their Fatherland, we in fact to some extent played our part in reducing the German resistance to the allies in Normandy after D-Day.

We were to later learn that the garrison in the Bailiwick was deemed no threat to the allies and it was assumed, despite having no proof, that we were on friendly terms with our occupiers and so there was no rush for our liberation as we would come to no harm in the meantime.

We badly needed supplies of medicine and clothing; how soon would be receive them after the liberation? What about money? We hadn't even seen Sterling banknotes or coins for ages. Would the Reichsmarks we used be worthless?

May 8th

H.M.S. Bulldog and others were anchored south of the Hanois Lighthouse, south-west of Guernsey on May 8th 1945.

It was expected that the top General would go to H.M.S. Bulldog, but it was instead a Junior Naval Officer, Lieutenant Zimmerman who was sent.

Apparently quite the Nazi fanatic, he gave the Hitler salute to the British officers even though Hitler was now dead and the war in Europe over.

The British relayed to him that there would be unconditional surrender of the German forces on the island, with no armistice conditions.

Zimmerman warned the British that they had no permission to stay in their current position in the waters and that the ships would soon be blown up. Mindful of the massive guns of the Mirus Battery, the Bulldog did move further over.

However before anything could escalate, the German High Command signed the unconditional surrender and the war was brought to an end.

As the German troops in Guernsey could no longer threaten the British ships, it was decided to move the vessels further in towards St Peter Port.

Liberation

On May 9th, General Heine boarded H.M.S. Bulldog and signed the unconditional surrender. Before he left, the swastika flag on the boat that brought him was replaced with the rightful much superior white ensign.

Brigadier Snow landed in St Peter Port accompanied by 35 men of the Royal Engineers, including some Guernsey men. They received a tumultuous reception, with union flags that had been hidden for nearly five years aired enthusiastically.

At 2pm on the steps of Elizabeth College, Brigadier Snow read the Royal Proclamation giving him the power of Military Commander. Not surprisingly there was a large number of people there to witness the momentous and unforgettable event.

Unfortunately, I missed all of this entirely.

I had gone into town on May 8th as we were led to believe that would be the day of our Liberation. It wasn't and we were left at the end of that day not knowing when it would be.

I did, however, go into town on May 10th and buy lots of flags to adorn the front of our house.

I still celebrate Liberation Day each year, along with the population of Guernsey, however as far as I am concerned the only true Liberation Day was that first one.

Sark

The Island of Sark, nine miles away from Guernsey and part of the Bailiwick, could not be liberated at the same time as us. A British officer did visit the island on May 10th and met the Dame of Sark. He explained to her that he couldn't spare any men for a while and would the Dame mind taking over the job of keeping an eye on the 275 German prisoners. It is said the Dame replied that having been left for five years, they could stand a few more days.

She was a determined woman and commanded the 275 German troops until they were finally removed from the island on May 17th. The sight of the British soldiers at this point was apparently welcomed by the Germans in comparison to the Dame of Sark's rule over them.

Removal

It took time for it to sink in that the Occupation was over. There was no curfew, no having to ride on the right-hand side of the road; freedom.

Soon after Liberation Day, Mother, Stepfather and I were on our front lawn chatting to neighbours when a few men of the Liberation troops appeared. They spoke to us for a while and one reached into the top pocket of his tunic and handed me a packet of biscuits. It was a gesture I shall never forget.

It was lovely to see soldiers dressed in khaki, smart, healthy and friendly. A contrast to the horrible grey, untidy, unhealthy ones we had been accustomed to seeing.

To be truly free, the unwelcome enemy had to be removed as quickly as possible. With thousands of them, it could have taken quite a while but thankfully this was not the case.

A large ship was anchored in Pembroke Bay in the North and at low tide the front opened up and a gangplank was lowered. The defeated soldiers were marched into the ship and taken off to camps in the U.K.

Even though we were now free to go where we wanted, there were still areas that remained out-of-bounds. The bays, cliffs and similar areas were still mined and dangerous. Over 70,000 mines had been planted on the island and the approaches to St Peter Port and the North.

As it was the garrisons that had deposited them, it was only fair that they were the ones to remove them. 1500 of them were asked to remain in order to carry out this task.

Thankfully, the Germans were efficient and organised; they knew exactly where the mines were and removed them. Surprisingly, only one was killed in the process.

De-fortifying the rest of the island took quite a bit longer; dismantling all the guns around the island including the four massive ones at Mirus Battery which were so thick they had to be cut before disposal for scrap.

A Fortune in Metal

A few days after the soldiers were removed from the large garrison at Castle Cornet, a schoolmate and I decided to have a look around. There was no one to be seen.

The anti-aircraft guns were still in position. In the building that became the Maritime Museum the Germans had deposited weapons and other items. There was a mass of German helmets.

I didn't know it at the time but these were going to become collector's items. Even today adverts appear in the local paper offering £100 for a single German helmet. It seems that if I had collected up the thousands of helmets that were there I could now be living a life of luxury! Several of them actually ended up dumped off Alderney.

Evacuees

We hadn't been able to contact any of our friends or relatives that had left the island at the beginning of the Occupation.

We had only received two messages from my Mother's sister and her two daughters. We knew that English towns were being bombed, so no messages might mean that no one was left to send them. It was very worrying.

It wasn't until after the Liberation that a letter was delivered from my Aunt. They were living in Leeds and were well. She had worked in a factory and Ada, her eldest, was a teacher in a school whilst Mildred worked in a clothes shop.

Returning the evacuees to the island was a much larger and more difficult problem than the original shipping out in June 1940 as instead of moving them from a small place to a much larger one, 20,000 people who were scattered over the country had to be gathered together to ship home.

Because of the war, there were fewer ships meaning that the task took weeks or months. The British Government needed to know if each person had a house and job to go back to. Because of the severe winter in 1944, with no fuel coming into the island, soldiers burnt furniture, doors and even floor boards to keep warm and many houses were left unfit for purpose.

Many who had no house to come back to and had employment and a place in the U.K. were in no hurry to return. My aunt later told us that if they hadn't had a nice big house that was in a fit state to return to, they would have remained in Leeds.

Others couldn't wait to return. My now wife, Gwyneth, was only 6 years old when she was evacuated with Forest Primary School. She said that it took 14 hours to get to England. Once there they continued on to

Cheadle Hulme near Manchester. For the vast majority of Guernsey children, travelling by train was a completely new experience.

Her parents stayed behind for a while as her father had his own tomato business but they soon realised they had made a terrible mistake in allowing their young daughter to leave. They abandoned their business and tried to find her.

Her father was a top-class golfer who played off scratch, winning many silver trophies. The last thing he did before they left for England was to bury his precious silver in the chicken run.

When they arrived in England they contacted the Red Cross and eventually they were able to tell them where their daughter was; she was staying with a woman and her middle-age son. She also related that she was very unhappy there as she had to do everything for herself. When she heard that her parents were coming to collect her, she was overjoyed. She even went as far as to kick the woman in the shins before they left!

Gwyneth enjoyed her remaining stay, now down in Plymouth with her aunt, even if they did have to withstand many bomb attacks. Guernsey would have possibly been safer! She met a local girl named Joan and they became firm friends. They took ballet lessons together and sometimes entertained American troops with their dance.

On returning to Guernsey, the first thing that her father did was to check if his buried silver was still there; it was. They were among the lucky few whose house was still intact and their possessions still there.

A cousin, Lloyd, was evacuated in 1940 at nine years old whilst his parents remained behind. They never heard from him, not knowing if he was dead or alive. That is, until he returned with his school in June 1945, now fourteen years old.

My uncle and aunt met the ship at the harbour, beyond thrilled at his safe return, although as they watched the various children disembark they could not see their son among them.

They couldn't recognise him; a teacher had to lead him over. He did not recognise them either; they were complete strangers. He told his teacher he wanted to go back to Manchester. Even now, after all these years, he still tells us that he regrets not being allowed to go back.

This was not an isolated incident.

Language Barriers

A great many of the children who were evacuated spoke the Guernsey Norman French fluently. Unfortunately not many people in the United Kingdom spoke the language of William the Conqueror. The Guernsey children had no choice but to speak the Anglo-Saxon languages instead.

Many who returned had forgotten how to speak their native tongue and could only speak English. Older ones who could still speak Guernsey French preferred to abandon it so it was left to the older 'remainers' like me to keep it alive.

I found it hard to understand the English spoken by many that returned. In several cases it differed significantly from the one I was learning. Phrases like 'big girl's blouse' and 'ee bah gum, lad' were perplexing. Whereas the English spoken by those returning from five years in Glasgow fooled me completely! Guernsey language has never been the same since!

Returning to Normal

There was a slow progress in restoring water, electricity and telephone service with the U.K.

Clothes and footwear arrived. I will never forget Mother taking me to Keylo's Men's Shop to buy a shirt. It wasn't the best quality and had a blue pattern on the outside and was white inside with a utility stamp. I didn't mind. It was the first new shirt I'd had in years.

Buses

After a while, much to our delight, buses were brought back into service. Only one trip to town and back. They had to be fairly new as they driven not by petrol but by charcoal. Large tanks were attached to the rear of the buses.

As the buses that had serviced our part of the Island were too old, newer buses had to be found, whereas the 'Bluebird' buses that had served the flatter North of the island were still fit for purpose.

The bus would depart from Town and begin its run from Pleinmont on the South-West Coast. It had to pass our home on the way there and I knew when, so I waited for it. The driver knew me and would stop to allow me to board. I could have a three mile ride without charge.

The bus took me to Town but I also needed to know exactly what time it left Town. If I was late, it meant a very long walk home!

Unfortunately, this comfortable mode of transport was soon abandoned through lack of charcoal.

'Our' Bus

We owned a large garage that before the war would house two large lorries and a car. It stood empty for most of the war, its vehicles commandeered by the occupying forces.

In late 1944, however, when we were allowed to return to our house, Mr Watson asked to hide one of his buses there. He had run a bus service before the war that had been known as 'the Greys' because of the bus colour. Step-Father gave him permission and I was delighted to see it there.

I spent a lot of time sitting in the driver's seat and working the controls. Near the driver's seat was a lever that opened and closed the door when pulled. I did this repeatedly with great aplomb.

After the war, Mr Watson repossessed his bus and I was very sorry to see it go.

Our car outside the large garage in question.

The Dutchman

Soon after the occupation began, a Dutch National approached our new rulers and said that he could provide them with all the vegetables and fruit they would need. He told them that his buildings were inadequate and a larger one would have to be built. He needed their assistance in building it and he had to have their backing to requisition other people's glasshouses.

He received help from the Germans to build a very large shed in cast iron with a veranda to protect carts when it rained and a long platform shaped so that many carts could be filled at once. Many strong horses were brought from France and used with the carts as their main form of transport.

The large shed is still there as I'm writing this, in La Rue de L'Epinel in the Forest Parish, without the veranda.

By taking over many vineries, including ours, and not paying rent, it's not a surprise that he became the most unpopular man on the island.

He gathered a large local workforce to grow the vegetables and another to fill the carts. Quite often I would go to see the carts being loaded and sometimes I was given melon and other fruits in season.

One day I went and could not see any carts to be loaded. What I did see was a parking area across the road which had been spread with stones and boys were picking up and throwing those stones at the two sons of the owner, stood under the veranda. The two young boys were too little to return the stones aggressively enough.

I decided to help them. I returned the stones rapidly and with great force and accuracy. The group of boys admitted defeat and left the battlefield, hurling abuse at me. They shouldn't be blaming the sons for their father's behaviour.

This was not a one-off occurrence. On another occasion I was passing their home, which bordered the road, when boys from the garden opposite flung lumps of hard soil into their garden.

Again the boys were making valiant efforts to return the missiles but they fell short of their target.

"Once more into the breach!" was my war-cry, as I mounted the steps into their garden and began steadily returning the lumps on their behalf. Again, it wasn't too long before the antagonists gave up.

The mother of the boys, a Guernsey woman, had seen what I had done and invited me inside where we all had a small square of chocolate. A rare delight with a taste I had long forgotten!

On Liberation Day, the Dutchman hoisted a union flag on his flag pole. The Rector of the Parish Church, Reverend Finey, whom I knew well from choir, was a lovely man and a true gentleman. However, when he saw that flag, flying where it should not be, he charged down the road to confront the culprit. If the flag was not removed, he wouldn't be held responsible for his actions! The flag was taken down and did not make a reappearance.

It was hoped that the Dutchman would be asked to leave and face recriminations along with the black marketers, however it is believed that by paying a very large tax bill he was allowed to remain and continue a reduced business.

However the growers whose greenhouses he had requisitioned, including us, never did get any rent.

His two sons, on the other hand, were abused relentlessly and were soon sent to England to pursue their studies.

The Honourable Thing

There were women in Guernsey who had children with the officers stationed in the island. Many waited for them to return once they were able.

One woman comes to mind who waited for an officer who never returned, leading to her immigrating to Australia.

There were some Germans who returned once they were released from the prisoner of war camps, to do the honourable thing.

One such man married a woman who owned a restaurant in St Peter Port. It was a very popular eating place and did a roaring trade for years to come. Before we were married my wife and I would go there twice a week. There was often a queue but whenever we were spotted we were allowed to bypass it. Whether he knew I had been here during the Occupation, I will never know but he always looked after us well.

An Odd Thing to Say?

In conclusion, although you might find it an odd things to say, I believe that it was somewhat a good thing that the Germans occupied our islands during World War II.

Firstly, because if they had not been here we may not have survived the duration of the war.

Secondly, in making Guernsey a fortress, the coast of Normandy was much weaker and easier to take on D-Day than if Rommel had had his way.

Would I Have Preferred Evacuation?

This is a question I often get asked and it is one I cannot answer.

I enjoyed remaining in Guernsey, yes, especially because I survived it unscathed. But a preference is something that cannot be determined without experiencing both sides.

I did learn a great deal of how to survive with little food, few friends and not many toys. I got to know myself very well and that means I can enjoy my own company as much as anyone else's – I do enjoy good company after all!

Truthfully, for me, it certainly was A Quiet War.

Post-War Years

Finally a Sports Day

In June 1945, the euphoria of being liberated and free still lingered in the air. However, there was still the little business of school to occupy my time.

We hadn't had a sports day since 1939. Brother Victor told us that we deserved a good one. Our playing field was still in a terrible mess but he was not deterred.

How he did it is still not known but he managed, with the help of the influential Old Boys, to secure the use of the magnificent Elizabeth College sports field.

On the day even the weather joined in; the sun shone and the smell of freshly mown grass filled the air.

The Upper Boys School were issued with white shorts and long white trousers whilst large berets, Tom-O-Slanter, adorned our heads in the school colours of red and blue. This is what we wore whilst displaying our well-practised physical exercises.

Once over, these outer clothes were removed to reveal our running gear; a white vest with red binding and white shorts.

The last race was with bicycles that had the spokes of the wheels threaded with coloured paper and whilst that was fun, the real highlight was drinking a glass of cool squash; 'Or-Lem' I believe it was called. That was certainly worth waiting five years for.

This brought to an end my marvellous time at Les Vauxbelets College.

It was holiday time and I was thoroughly enjoying myself. I would spend time at Raymond's farm and we would wonder all over the parish and explores the cliffs at leisure after five long years of them being covered with enemy mines.

I would cycle into town and marvel how shops that had remained mostly empty for so long were now filled with goods that we hadn't seen since the war began. Chocolate and sweets appeared but we were only allowed a small amount as they weren't quite freely available yet; ration books restricted the amounts we could buy.

My trips into town were made much easier by the return of the bus service and the 'Greys' bus from our garage was used once more.

Things were finally returning to normal.

Elizabeth College

One day I shall never forget began with Mother informing me that she had made an appointment to meet the Principal of Elizabeth College; the Reverend William Henry Goodenough Milnes, no less.

He was a large man with a moustache turning to grey and was very pleasant as we were ushered into his study. He asked Mother questions about my education, she in turn telling him about the Grammar Schools and Les Vauxbelets College.

He appeared fairly satisfied with these credentials and after a worrying pause in which Mother reassured him that she would be paying the fees, he beamed a broad smile and I was welcomed in.

He gave me the number 4502 and informed us what I was to wear, including the distinguished school cap. I was now a proud pupil of a school founded in 1563 on the order of Her Majesty Queen Elizabeth I but unfortunately I had to wait until September for the school to re-open.

The Forest Primary School opened a fortnight earlier and I was anxious to see what the pupils looked like. Would I recognise anyone? They had all been away from the island for years.

I didn't. They were all complete strangers.

On my first day at Elizabeth College, I cycled in on Mother's gift of a new bicycle - with gears!

We all assembled in the hall and had to wait to learn which form we were in. Mine was IV A and Captain Chambers was the form master.

The room was on the first floor overlooking the harbour. Captain Chambers greeted us and it was at this point I experienced my first disappointment; he was wearing his black gown but there was no mortarboard in sight. I was shocked at this omission. In all the books with English Public Schools that I had read the masters had worn them.

Coloured postcard of Elizabeth College, St Peter Port
© Guernsey Museums & Galleries

Looking smart in my school uniform

Training Corps

The part of our curriculum that I was really looking forward to was what had been known pre-war as the Officer Training Corps (O.T.C.) but was now Junior Training Corps (J.T.C.)

It wasn't compulsory but we had to join; the boys who indicated that they had no intention of joining were soon urged and even pressured into submitting.

We were issued with a khaki uniform and this was when I received my second disappointment at Elizabeth College.

Before the Occupation, I was on the same school bus as a college boy, a very nice chap called Bob Gill. Once a week he wore the army uniform complete with a very smart peaked cap. That was what I was looking forward to.

Whilst the uniform was still smart, it now included a beret rather than a peaked cap and strange though it may seem, I felt I had been let down.

I enjoyed the army training twice a week. In July, those of us who were interested went to England for a fortnight of training. The first, in 1946 was at the Royal Military Academy at Sandhurst. There were many schools from the South-West of England and we all slept in tents. I had a marvellous time there.

The next year we went to Aldershot and I didn't enjoy it anywhere near as much but the last year I attended, in 1948, we went to Warminster in Wiltshire and I was in charge of the tent.

We took the school band and it led the way on route marches. Our drums had been taken to Germany during the Occupation but had been returned, the Tudor Coat of Arms along with our school named emblazoned on them. It was a proud moment.

The J.T.C. Uniform

The Beauty of Church

After the Liberation, I continued to go to Forest Parish Church and take part in the choir. Our congregation had shrunk, mainly because the Methodists could now use their own church once more and others presumably because their prayers for the end of the war had been answered and they felt no further need to attend.

In contrast, our Sunday School only had two members during the Occupation but many returning children joined and we were soon well in double figures.

They were all new faces to me and one memorable Sunday, a young girl joined. She sat in the pew in front of me with long hair resting neatly on her shoulders.

I have to admit that I was not listening to a word Reverend Finey was saying. My eyes were fixed on the lovely hair in front of me and my mind wondered what her face looked like... Would it match the beauty of her hair?

At the end of the lesson she stood and as she turned towards me I confirmed that her face was indeed a beautiful complement to her fine hair. She was the prettiest girl I had ever seen.

I asked the boy next to me if he knew her name but only got a curt 'no' in response. I had a feeling that he did in fact know her but was refusing to tell me.

Outside the church, a few stayed and chatted. I saw that the girl was very popular with the others and I observed that they were all at the Parish School. I was completely ignored, so much so that I stopped going to Sunday School as I felt unable to bear the situation.

I did continue to attend services as a choir boy and also joined the team of bell ringers. Even though I was only a school boy at the time, I was given the heaviest bell.

With these duties and my new school, I was kept fully occupied.

Monday; lessons all day.

Tuesday; more lessons.

Wednesday; lessons.

Thursday; morning lessons, afternoon football or hockey training.

Friday; lessons followed by J.T.C. (having to wear full uniform all afternoon)

Saturday; morning lessons, afternoon football or hockey matches at the college fields.

Sunday; church morning and evening.

All of this left me no time to wander the parishes in pursuit of the delightful young girl who occupied my thoughts. Disaster!

Through Fifth to Sixth Form

To my great relief I passed the Oxford and Cambridge School Certificate in Fifth Form at college with form master Mr Thompson and was allowed to join Sixth Form. Mother even bought me a gold watch in congratulations.

Even so, Mother had been making greater plans. She wanted me to work in a bank and had previously approached our Rector, Reverend Finey, who was a trustee of the Savings Bank.

He told Mother to return once I passed my certificate and he'd see what he could do. Now that I had done so, he told her about a vacancy at the bank that was mine if I wanted it.

I turned it down. I didn't feel that working in a bank, especially as in those days promotion was slow, was my idea of an interesting career. Two days later another boy left my form and took that position, eventually becoming manager.

Naturally, Mother was disappointed at my decision but I was not rebuked and she allowed me to continue my studies.

In the Sixth Form we were allowed to choose a subject we wished to pursue. I chose Foreign Languages; English, French and Spanish. Three other boys also chose Languages but preferred German to Spanish. I, however, had had quite enough of German during the Occupation and definitely did not want more. That being said, not wanting to be alone, I did reluctantly join the others.

A Beautiful Meeting

One morning in spring 1947, I was on the bus on the way to school when it stopped near the airport and the very same girl I had seen at church mounted the steps into the bus. She wore a maroon school uniform and so I learned that her parents had sent her to a very posh school, known as the Guernsey High School for Girls, only a stone's throw from Elizabeth College.

Sometimes I would see her out with friends or on the bus but our interactions never got further than the odd "hello".

It was a Sunday after leaving the vestry in cassock and surplice, heading towards the stalls, that I saw her seated amongst the female members of the choir. I met her eyes and she smiled. Thank the Good Lord!

After the service I changed as quickly as possible to be in with a chance of meeting her when the Rector pulled me aside for a word. When I managed to get away, I grabbed my bicycle and headed in the direction she would have gone. I couldn't see her anywhere.

Eventually I saw her a distance ahead, walking slowly and looking back repeatedly. I caught up with her and dismounted to walk with her. I learned her name was Gwyneth.

This went on for weeks, Sunday mornings and Friday evenings after choir practise. We became good friends but I had a nasty feeling that would be as far as it would go.

One Sunday soon after these thoughts began to form, I reached my pew and looked across the aisle to the soprano section, as usual, to find she wasn't there. I thought she might not be well.

This hope was soon dashed as weeks and months passed with no sign of her. I no longer saw her on the bus. I was told she had left school and was pursuing a career in Haute Couture...and that she had been seen in the company of a boyfriend.

I was heartbroken. It was clearly game over.

Driving

Life had to go on. On my seventeenth birthday, Mother arranged for me to have a proper driving lesson.

I arrived in my school J.T.C. uniform and Mr Bougourd, my instructor, was very pleased with my first attempt. He had sold Mother and Step-Father a new Morris 10. He could tell I had been practising in it and by the second lesson he told me he would make an appointment for me to take the test.

I passed and was able to drive the Morris 10 on the roads.

Important Decisions

Now that I was approaching adulthood, I had to make decisions for my future. I originally wanted to be a teacher and Mother found this acceptable but by the end of 1948, I had begun to doubt that I would be any good.

With a possible three years of university ahead after which I reckoned I would be twenty three years of age before I could earn a penny, I decided I wanted to leave school and follow a different path.

Tomato Growing was big business at this time and growers were earning a small fortune. As I already owned a vinery, which we let out and used the resulting money to pay my college fees, I decided that my future would be in horticulture.

This was my first major decision and the best.

Working hard in my vinery, with plentiful fruit on the vines.

My First Pay Day

I took over the vinery in 1949, Mother writing a cheque for £250 and together we took it to Barclays Bank in Fountain Street. We had an appointment with the manager and when he saw the size of the cheque I was warmly invited to be a member of their bank.

At the age of 18 years, I was going to be my own boss and run my own business.

I took to the role with great enthusiasm and in May 1949 I began to export tomatoes. In that month I received my first cheque to the value of £16-10 Shillings.

I took the bus into St Peter Port and deposited the cheque at my bank. This was followed by a visit to the bicycle shop. My friend Raymond had bought a sports bike and told me that they had only one left. It had low handlebars, three speeds and a dynamo. It was green and white and an absolute joy to ride.

A Reunion

I was still in the Forest Church Choir and one autumn Sunday that year, something happened which would change the direction of my life.

To my astonishment, in the female section of the choir once again sat the charming young woman I thought I would never see again.

After service, I rushed outside to find her waiting at the gate. She admired my new bike.

As we walked towards her home, I asked her why she had re-joined the choir to which she replied; "I wanted to see you."

Those were words that I never would have thought I'd hear from her lips.

From then on she was a regular attendee of the morning service and choir practices. However as the daylight hours were getting shorter and she said that she didn't like walking home from work, I thought I might borrow Mother's Morris 10 and pick Gwyneth up at the bus stop and drive her home through the dark lanes.

I stopped the car alongside her, I opened the passenger door and offered her a lift. The interior of the car was lit and when she saw me, she accepted my invitation graciously.

Success.

Stolen Away

All was going well and it was now spring 1951. I was still doing my taxi routine, now in my own car; a new Morris Minor.

One day I waited as usual but Gwyneth didn't appear. I thought she might be unwell so I drove towards her house with no sight of her but luckily I did see one of her friends, named Ruth. I asked her if she could visit Gwyneth's house and let her know I wanted to see her.

I waited in my car in the lane when the passenger door suddenly swung open and Gwyneth slipped in. She wasn't her usual smiling self.

It was then that she told me they were moving; her family were to live in Jersey.

This was the last thing I wanted to hear. We sat in silence.

When she had to leave, she asked me if I would write to her if she sent me her address, to which I readily agreed. I then remained in my car for a while, unable to believe what I had heard.

Eventually I forced myself to move; I had work still to do... I had to check the glasshouse boilers were maintaining the heat the plants needed.

The following week a letter arrived from the other island.

Gwyneth had kept her word.

We exchanged letters every week and in June, I told Mother that I would like to go to Jersey for a few days and asked if she would look after the plants. We found someone to help her pick and pack the tomatoes and I booked airline tickets and a room at the Woodville Hotel.

Once in Jersey, I made sure to have breakfast early so that I could walk Gwyneth to her place of employment and home again in the afternoon. In the evenings we would take a stroll or watch a film. It was an unforgettable few days.

The beautiful Gwyneth, looking radiant as ever.

Between a Rock and a Hard Place

I found it hard to concentrate on my business.

I would often take walks between work and church services. On one such occasion I was stood at the top of La Corbières headland, watching people down below walking on the rocks.

To make the most of the lovely day, I decided to climb down and walk along the rocks eastwards as far as Le Fond du Val where there was a ladder to climb up again. It was only a mile long. I reckoned I could do it easily and still make church for Evensong.

Unfortunately I didn't take into account that the walk wouldn't be straight. There was no way I was going to make it in time after clambering up and down rocks. I decided the only solution was to climb directly up. It was a long way but it didn't seem too difficult.

It started well and I was within ten feet of the top where the hard rock gave way to soil. I was stuck. I found myself unable to go further up and a very long, tricky climb down. My feet were fortunately on solid rock but I could not reach anything to help myself over the top.

I looked down and found myself surprisingly calm. It was a long way back down but I noticed a rock formation in the shape of a horse's saddle about halfway that would stop my descent if I did end up sliding downwards.

I decided to give one more attempt at climbing up before giving up on my ascent. Unfortunately every small piece of rock I tried came away in my hands and every piece of bush snapped. It was no good. To make matters worse, my legs had begun to feel weak and shake. There was only one reasonable solution; "Please God help me!" I cried.

Immediately I gained a response. My legs felt less like jelly and it felt like a strong hand grabbed the shirt on my back. The next rock I grabbed held firm and the scrub remained unbroken. I made those last few feet in record time.

By some miracle I managed to make it to church in time and thanked the Good Lord for helping me. Needless to say, I never attempted such folly again.

A Visit to London

Also in 1951, as a distraction, my friend Raymond suggested that we should visit the Great Exhibition in London.

The tomato season was virtually over at this point, so I agreed. I got my Morris Minor onto the ship to Southampton and we drove up to London.

We found accommodation near Russell Square and enjoyed two days in London. Raymond then asked if I would mind taking him to Kent to visit a friend. I can't say I was overjoyed at this idea but I took him all the same. His friend lived in a small village that took ages to find.

When I left him there, it was dark and I was not used to driving under such conditions. How I managed to find London again, let alone Russell Square, I shall never know! Three days later I repeated the trip to collect Raymond and travel back to Southampton.

I spent those three days in London, alone. I wasn't worried, having spent a lot of time on my own during the Occupation but London was quite different.

The Best News

Just a few weeks later I went to Jersey to stay with Gwyneth and her parents. On one of our walks, I said something that was to change everything.

Taking a deep breath, I blurted; "Let's be serious."

Her reaction was immediate. With a beaming smile that lit up the night, she replied, "I've been waiting years to hear you say that."

I have to say that I had been worried I wouldn't receive such a joyous response.

We walked home with a spring in both our steps. My return to Guernsey was heart-breaking but being a Guernseyman and an Old Elizabethan, I put on a brave face.

It was shortly after this that a letter arrived, postmarked from Jersey. I could not believe what I read once it was opened. I rubbed my eyes. There was no mistaking it; Gwyneth and her parents were returning to Guernsey! I felt I had won top prize! Having her back on home soil was a joy.

We went to the jewellers in the High Street and picked out an engagement ring, costing £50. Mr Bachmann, a very nice man, congratulated me on our choice of ring and my choice of partner. The engagement was made official on Christmas Day and my life was to be completely transformed.

Now my fiancée.

Working Hard to Reap Rewards

In 1952, Gwyneth found employment in a shop selling top of the range clothes for women whilst I was kept busy getting the glasshouses ready for the new season.

Sometimes I would get time to collect her from town and other times she would take the bus to the stop near the vinery.

Occasionally she would bring me chocolates, still rationed at this time, for which she used coupons from her ration book. Naturally, I shared them with her.

I worked hard to have a profitable season as we needed money for our wedding, furniture and other items.

Thankfully, 1953 was also successful and this enabled us to pay for our wedding; finally fixed for September 9th.

On Our Wedding Day

The ceremony took place in the Forest Parish Church and the service was conducted by Reverend Finey. We chose the United Kingdom for our honeymoon and took the Morris Minor across to Southampton.

We went to Plymouth, where Gwyneth spent five years during the war, then on to Honiton where we intended to spend the night.

Unfortunately, when we got to the hotel it was full. The owner was very apologetic and when she found out that we were on our honeymoon, she rang a friend who owned a small hotel in the country.

There was one room vacant and we immediately told her we'd take it. The downside? It was twenty miles away and it was getting dark; there was little time to waste.

We were given directions and set off. After about ten miles, it was pitch-black. I hoped we were on the right road. I didn't say so but I had visions of us spending the night in the car.

We were driving uphill for a very long time and the car began to struggle. All of a sudden, the engine stopped completely. I couldn't get it to go.

Gwyneth suggested I go to the large house nearby for help.

I returned in a much better frame of mind; "This is it!" I told her.

The universe must have agreed with me because the car started first time and I drove it into the yard. It was a miracle that the car stopped where it did.

Our trip continued on to Wales, up the Wye Valley and Caernarfon then on to Neston to visit a cousin who taught in a school nearby. She had been unable to attend our marriage service and was overjoyed to see us. She gave us a cup of school tea which was actually drinkable!

For the second week we drove down to London, enjoying a lovely time before heading home and straight to our new residence.

Homes & Holidays

Mother had by now bought the same semi-detached house that she and I had lived in pre-war for my family to live in. Ironically we took over the very half Mother and I had lived in then.

Gwyneth soon joined me in our business, leaving her old place of employment. The vinery was increasing in size, as was our family; in September 1954 our daughter, Michelle, was born.

It wasn't long before we needed extra help at the vinery; I was a very professional tomato grower and I had a heavy, high quality crop in 1955 that gave the best ever financial return by far.

With business going well, I decided it was time to try and repay, in some small way, the sacrifices Mother had made for me in looking after me and turning me into the man I now am.

She had often intimated that she would love to visit the town of Nice in the South of France and taking her to visit seemed the best way.

Gwyneth thought it was an excellent idea and Mother was thrilled. Step-Father remained behind; he said that at seventy five years of age he would not be able to survive fourteen days in France!

We chose the last fortnight of September and took their lovely light blue Morris Oxford as our old Morris Minor would have been unable to cope with the French Alps.

It took Mother, Gwyneth, Michelle and I five days to reach La Côte d'Azur and Nice. Mother enjoyed speaking to the staff in French but the hotel was not to her liking. She found she much preferred Menton near the Italian border.

It was here that Michelle learned to walk, only a few days past her first birthday. A wonderful end to what we all agreed was a fortnight well spent.

Gwyneth and I visited Europe again in 1957, including the Italian Riveria as well as France. This time visiting Paris where we reached summit of the Eiffel Tower and experienced an unforgettable drive down Les Champs Elysées and around the Arc de Triumph.

Our only hiccup this time was that Gwyneth was three months pregnant and was not allowed to drive on recommendation from her doctor, so luckily a friend of ours who helped pick and pack our tomatoes offered to split the driving with me.

In February 1958 our first son, Paul, was born and we made the decision to build a new house on the grounds of the vinery, meaning there would be no more holidays for a while.

Mother, Gwyneth & Michelle in France

Gwyneth, Michelle & I in Monte Carlo.

New Phases

The plot that we chose for our new home was exactly the same that my father had chosen all those years ago.

The crop looked promising and the bank allowed me to have an overdraft to cover the cost of the house. Building began in September and before we knew it the house was ready to move into in Easter 1959.

Carpets, tiles floors, curtains and an aga had been installed which all added to the cost. Our expenses were also increased by the birth of our second son, Martin, in September 1960. Holidays remained on hold.

Our three children; Paul, Michelle & Martin.   *Martin & Paul*

Unfortunately, in November of that year, Step-Father died at eighty years of age. However Mother found a companion in another woman who had also survived her husband; Mrs Robert. They spoke to each other exclusively in Guernsey French and she cleaned the home and cooked meals. This gave time for Mother to look after crops in the glasshouses. It was an ideal partnership.

Life continued in comfortable fashion until, in the 1970s, a massive change occurred in the Horticultural Industry.

Out with the Old, in with the New

Competition from Holland in the tomato industry meant that changes in our industry were needed.

Growers were advised to remove their old glasshouses with wide wooden supports and narrow panels of glass and replace them with those of slim metal with much wider glass.

Many growers followed this advice but many had to borrow money in order to do so. Unfortunately, loans were a struggle to repay when interest rates went through the roof. Oil prices also rose from £50 for 1000 gallons to £360.

Several found themselves unable to continue and lost not only their vineries but also their houses.

Fortunately, I had abandoned tomatoes for flowers. The glasshouses I already had were perfectly adequate for roses and freesias and therefore I avoided having to repay a large loan.

Gwyneth amongst the numerous blooms in our glasshouse

With this move proving another success, I asked Gwyneth if perhaps she would like her own business as a dressmaker. With her great enthusiasm two large rooms were added to the house that would be hers to use as she needed.

A small advert was placed in the local press for three days. Her pleasant attitude and high quality, professional work meant she never had to advertise again.

Her business thrived through word of mouth, with many titled women among her clientele. She also added curtain-making to her repertoire to diversify further.

As for my business, I had gathered a gang of housewives wanting occasional work to supplement their incomes …but then the 1980s brought more trouble.

A Downward Turn

The 1980s is not a decade that I look back on with any affection. It was the beginning of the decline of commercial growing in glasshouses.

The markets in the United Kingdom were being flooded with vast amounts of flowers from warmer countries. Their flowers were grown outdoors and didn't need expensive heating, with their wages well below ours too.

I abandoned the glasshouses Father had built and as a result my workforce was reduced. I decided to seek part-time employment but was unsuccessful, partly because of my age. It appeared that I was over-qualified for some and under-qualified for others.

I removed the old glasshouses and used the land to grow carnations. This was a disastrous decision that lost me £15,000 over two years.

1986 was the true low point of that decade. My mother passed on. She was four weeks short of her eighty-sixth birthday.

Her eyesight had deteriorated so much that she could no longer watch television and a fear of operations and hatred of hospitals kept her from having the cataracts surgery she needed. It was a massive stroke that ended her life.

She was a strong woman, always active, and being confined to sitting in a chair all day was very hard for her to bear.

The small positive of this period was that I did manage to find part-time employment in a large rose nursery towards the end of the 1980s but it took some getting used to after being my own boss for forty years. I felt my talents were being wasted.

Thankfully, Gwyneth's business, on the other hand, was flourishing. The quality of her work was admired by many.

It was clear I needed a change in my life.

A New Job

In 1992, my prayers were answered. I met a friend, a top civil servant, who knew of a part-time job I could do. I could speak English and French and had a well-known knowledge of Guernsey. This meant that there was a vacancy at Castle Cornet that would suit me.

I sent in a form, signed by my friend, and received an interview. Mrs Cole, the Director of the Museums at the time, welcomed me and asked how well I knew the man who signed my form.

I told her that we were near-neighbours who often popped round for a chat and that we played badminton together.

I got the job.

On my first day a Castle Cornet, I was smartly dressed. This was also new to me! I left home clean and tidy and returned home clean and tidy; a great contrast to the preceding forty years working with soil and plants as a grower.

I was on duty in the largest building, the Maritime Museum, working four days a week; Monday, Wednesday, Friday and Sunday one week and the opposite days the next.

It didn't take me long to get into the swing of things, welcoming visitors and answering all manner of questions. Many visitors were French and I was able to use my command of the language regularly, to their delight.

In 1995, things changed and I was to work in a different one of the five museums each day I was on duty. This added enormously to my knowledge of the history of the Castle, some of which was 800 years old.

Open University

In 1999, I decided that I wanted to improve my French further, so I took a course with the Open University. I was intrigued to see an assessment of my knowledge.

I thoroughly enjoyed the experience; even more so when I got overall results of Distinction.

I only did the one year but had I been ten years younger, I would have done the following two to receive a diploma.

Dear Mr Gallienne,

You will by now have received your overall course result for your study of L120, Ouverture, completed in 1998. This letter is supplementary to your overall course result in that it reports in more detail your achievements in the Writing and Speaking outcomes in the continuous and End-of-course Assessments, and in the Language and Grammar assessed via the CMAs.

The outcomes were assessed on the course by applying the assessment grids shown in your Assessment Books for the TMAs and for the preparation materials for the End-of-course Assessment.

The performance levels that you achieved were:

	Continuous Assessment	End-of-course Assessment
Writing	90%	86%
CMAs	88%	--
Speaking	93%	85%

Your overall achievement has been assessed on a six point scale, described as follows:

Category	Description
Distinction	- achievement at the highest level expected on this course; demonstrates the ability to progress to the next course in the Diploma programme.
Very Good	- achievement at a high level of proficiency; demonstrates the ability to progress to the next course in the Diploma programme.
Good	- achievement which demonstrates sufficient proficiency to progress to the next course in the Diploma programme.
Operational	- performance which merits a pass and which demonstrates the ability to understand and communicate effectively in a variety of straightforward situations.
Survival	- achievement which is below the standard required by the course but which nevertheless indicates ability to understand and communicate in some straightforward situations.
Non-operational	- insufficient evidence to indicate that understanding or communication would be achieved.

Your overall achievements were assessed as: Distinction.

I wish you every success in the future.

Yours Sincerely

X.P. Hassan
L120 Examination and Assessment Board

A Pause

With my new job, Gwyneth and I were finally able to resume our visits to France, with two short breaks a year.

This came to a halt in the spring of 2001 when concerns for Gwyneth's health and a hospital trip to Southampton discovered a hole in her heart that had been there since birth.

When the doctor discovered that she did ballet in her youth, had lifted thousands of tonnes of heavy tomato baskets, gave birth to three children and played badminton for forty years, he was shocked she hadn't had serious issues sooner; a 'miracle' he called it.

Luckily, the operation was a great success and we were home ten days later.

Since then, we have managed to hold our health enough to enjoy river cruises and short trips to France.

Fame at Last

It came as a great surprise when I received a telephone call from Penny Wark, a reporter for 'The Times' in London.

I was told that an American woman had visited Guernsey and written a book on the Occupation, titled 'The Guernsey Literary and Potato Peel Pie Society.'

She said that it was set to be a bestseller and 'The Times' was going to promote it in our part of the world. She wanted to interview people who had lived in Guernsey under German rule.

She came to our house along with another charming young lady who took my photograph. An article was published in 'The Times' on Friday 8th August 2008.

The book is now a bestseller and a film. I like to wonder if my photograph in 'The Times' helped it reach that height… I'm sure it's hard to say!

It never ceases to surprise that even seventy years after the event that interest in the Occupation is ever increasing.

And now...

At time of writing, I am still involved in Castle Cornet. Not as much as before but enough for me. I am an official Guide and do tours an average of eleven a month during the main season. Although most are conducted in English there are occasions where I can still use my French language to entertain French visitors as I first did many years prior.

I am also involved in the Living History Performances at the Castle; theatrical talks and sketches that portray elements and events from Guernsey's extensive history. To perfect my presentation, I am fortunate enough to have a talented seamstress for a wife. Gwyneth made me a splendid Tudor outfit with material that cost the earth - for anyone else the outfit would have been charged at £300. It is admired by many.

Gwyneth & I in our splendid historical outfits.

When I am not working at the Castle, I give talks to local schools about life during the Occupation, including my old school of Elizabeth College. Even visiting French schools have listened with rapt attention to my stories in their native tongue.

I find it extraordinary to think that all those years ago, while in Sixth Form myself, I decided to abandon thoughts of becoming a teacher because I felt that I wouldn't be any good at it. Yet today, I feel that I might have been successful in that field after all.

I am grateful that I have been allowed to continue working for so long, enjoying all my roles at the Castle. The numerous mentions of 'Fred's Tour' in positive reviews may have helped!

Invariably, while I am giving my tours and Living History Performances in all weathers, Gwyneth sits in the Refectory, chatting with visitors and drumming up interest with the same charm that brought clientele to her business. She could well be described as an honorary member of staff.

After finishing my work I join her in the Refectory and am habitually greeted by "Have you any money to pay for my coffee and cake?" I always pay up; we Guernseymen always look after our wives well.

It is appropriate to end this memoir with a question I am often asked; "Why are you still working at your age?"

Many years ago I read words written by Guy de Maupassant, the celebrated French poet:

'Vieillir n'est qu'une mauvaise habitude.
L'homme occupé n'a pas le temps de la prende.'

'Growing old is only a bad habit.
The busy man does not have time to take it.'

This I took as advice for life and I'm so very glad I did.

Appendix 1:

Horticulture in Guernsey

By Frederick Gallienne, 1997

ACCREDITATIONS

FRED GALLIENNE, CASTLE CORNET

Horticulture in Guernsey

In 1792, the first heated glasshouse was built in Guernsey. It is still in use and can be found in Candie Gardens. At that time, no one could have forseen what dramatic changes the glasshouse would bring. It changed the face of Guernsey and provided for a standard of living the ordinary man had never before imagined.

* * *

Vines

Farmers were the major landowners and it is they, above all others, who foresaw the potential of a heated glasshouse. Their business was stagnant and in order to expand, a product needed to be found which could be exported. Britain provided the obvious market because our established shipping route already existed. Also, successive Monarchs had granted the islanders certain privileges; no tariff would be levied on their produce.

Grapes were the first major crop to be grown for export with records of quantities first recorded in 1830. It was labour intensive, with gangs of young ladies seated on ladders hand-thinning the grapes with thin pointed scissors.

The sight of large bunches of ripe grapes - white and black - hanging gracefully from the vine was indeed a pleasant sight, exuding a romantic fragrance that can never be forgotten. Sadly, the area in grape production started to decline from the 1920's onwards. The growing of grapes in earlier times is the reason why holdings in the island are still referred to as vineries.

* * *

The Tomato

The introduction of the tomato, or love apple, as it was first known, was the main reason for the decline of the grape. Businessmen, unconnected with farming, saw the potential for investment. The rapid growth of the industry was staggering. Vast areas of land were covered with wood and glass.

A bigger labour force was needed, and many young men, fleeing from the depression in Britain, arrived to find work. They were closely followed by the Dutch. However, before they could work or even contemplate owning their own vinery, they needed residential qualifications. Marrying a Guernsey person was the obvious solution. A familiar story.

Many glasshouse workers took advantage of readily available loans and built one glasshouse, usually between 150 to 200 feet in length. A boiler pit was dug and a chimney built, Life was hard as they were obliged to continue with their employers. It meant getting up at dawn, climbing down a ladder into the boiler pit clinker out and stoke up the boiler. Clouds of sulphorous fumes surrounded him which brought huge bouts of coughing. Vents had to be opened by hand and during the lunch hour he watered the plants with a heavy hose. In the evening, he would tend to the plants. His wife was to play an important role in the venture. She would pick and grade the fruit.

After two or three years they were in a position to increase their holding to between 400 and 500 feet. This was sufficient for the man to give up his job and concentrate on his business. Many believe that this period epitomises the so-called 'Guernsey Way of Life'.

With so much land covered by glass, vast amounts of water were needed to sustain the plants. The Reservoir had not yet been built, so growers needed to find their own source of supply. Wells were dug and huge windmills built to pump the water into large tanks perched on tall stands.

* * *

Auxiliary Services

As the industry grew, so did other businesses. A large fleet of lorries carted coal to satisfy the insatiable appetite of the boilers; one to each glasshouse. Millions of wooden baskets were made and delivered to vineries. Once filled, they were then transported to the harbour and loaded onto cargo boats. Commission Agents sprung up and, for a fee, they would find markets in England and organise transport.

Competition in this field was fierce and for the supplier of sundries it was even more intense. Representatives of the firms visited the growers and worked hard to convince them that their products were best - fertilizers, pesticides, hoses, string etc. Free advise on how to best use the product was offered.

At the height of the tomato industry, 3,000 people worked in the glasshouses, and as many outside supporting it.

*   *   *

Flowers

In the 1960's, when returns for tomatoes fell, some growers resorted to double cropping. In the winter, flowers such as Freesias, Chrysanths and Iris were grown. In the 1970's, fuel prices rocketed and many growers began to concentrate on flowers. Freesias, Iris, together with the introduction of Carnations, could be grown all year round and the heating requirement was low. In the case of carnations, virtually nil. Roses which was a well-established crop by then, needed heating. However, with the introduction of new varieties and increased production, prices obtained were usually sufficient to sustain a heating programme. Flower growing today is in a relatively healthy state.

*   *   *

Employment in the Industry

The days when the industry employed thousands of staff have gone. From nearly 6,000 people in 1966 to just over 1,500 today. This is due in part to a steady fall in land use by the industry from a peak of 1,000 acres in 1966 to under 500 acres in 1995. The industry becoming increasingly labour efficient is also a contributory factor.

Nearly half of the present labour force is brought in from Madeira. Where the glasshouse once echoed to the sound of Guernsey French, today, Portugese is the predominant language heard.

* * *

Summary

The decline of the industry has been arrested, it is leaner and fitter than it has been for some time. The building of modern double-glazed glasshouses has meant increased production per acre. The industry is now highly mechanised and computerised.

As for tomatoes, the market is now dominated by the multiples. The Supermarket chains dictate what they want. There is now the cherry tomato, the beef tomato and the longer life tomato. Rumour has it, that genetic artists are working on a square tomato for sandwiches.

The housewife has become more aware of the effects of pesticides. They are no longer used. The grower has engaged a useful ally - the bumble bee - who gobbles up all the red spider, green fly and white fly as soon as they appear.

Where have all the glasshouses gone? Might well be suitable lyrics for a song, but it is a question often asked by visitors. The Guernsey donkey is a stubborn and resourceful creature, he will not let the industry die.

* * *

Appendix 2:

A Walk in Forest Parish

By Frederick Gallienne, 1997

NOTES ON A WALK TAKEN RECENTLY

Anyone travelling along the main road that cuts through the parish of the Forest may well be curious to know why it bears that name as there is little evidence of flora.

Starting at the bottom of Le Chêne hill and taking the lane that borders the hotel, one arrives at a track which leads to an area which contains acres of land with enough trees and vegetation to satisfy even the greediest herbivores. It is like stepping back in time. There are no cars and no buildings. All is still save the song of the birds and the relaxing sound of the stream as it flows gently over stones down to Petit Bôt Bay.

On some of the hedges the wall Pennywort are strong and tall as any to be seen anywhere. At the point, the trees bordering the track are so tall that they touch at the tips, giving one an impression of walking down the aisle of a Cathedral, especially when accompanied by the song of a congregation of wild birds.
This is the parish of the Forest - the land of my youth .

Ambling down the track awakened memories of the past. The short clump of Sycamores from which I had stolen a stout shoot to make a staff, now stretches into the sky. The rough track along which I had helped my parents push a heavy truck full of firewood during the occupation had hardly altered. I also found the very spot where in 1942, I had shot three Red Indians - aged 5¾ - with a single round. After a while, the track forks. If possible both should be explored, if not, the right hand one although longer, is well worth the effort.

The cliffs have their attraction and some of the views along them are spectacular, but the most relaxing and rewarding walk of all, in my opinion, is the one that starts at Le Chêne and ends at Petit Bôt. After sitting for a while overlooking the bay whilst taking some refreshment, visitors can catch the mini bus which will take them up the stiff mile long haul to Le Bourg and the main bus route.

*   *   *

About the Author

Fred Gallienne is a Guernseyman through and through; fluent in Guernésias, he ran his own horticultural business at eighteen years old before retiring after forty years and becoming an official Tour Guide at Castle Cornet in St Peter Port, Guernsey.

He still lives in his home island with his wife Gwyneth after having three wonderful children; Michelle, Paul & Martin.

This is his second publication, the first being a light-hearted novel set in Guernsey titled *The Harassment of Mr de Bré*.